LIKENING THE BOOK OF MORMON WAR CHAPTERS TO YOUR LIFE

LIKENING THE BOOK OF MORMON WAR CHAPTERS TO YOUR LIFE: A STUDY JOURNAL

MANDY AL-BJALY

This book is dedicated to my five stripling warriors, Casey, Rigel, Kamren, Eve, and Asher.

Table of Contents

Part II: Lessons from the War Chapters

"…for I did liken all scriptures unto us, that it might be for our profit and learning." (Nephi, 1 Nephi 19:23)

Introduction

Nearly 11 years ago, I began teaching a Book of Mormon class for mothers. I learned and grew through studying the scriptures more thoroughly and sharing thoughts with the women in my class.

My favorite chapters to facilitate were what latter-day saints call the "war chapters." This surprised me because in the past I hadn't liked Captain Moroni (the main hero) and thought the war chapters were boring and had nothing to do with my life. How wrong I was! For the first time in my life, I realized how valiant Captain Moroni was, and how these chapters can be likened to the spiritual wars in each of our lives. If only I had known and understood that when I was a youth! That's when I got the idea to write this book.

As I began researching and writing almost eight years ago, I did so with my then preteen son in mind. I felt a spiritual call to help him, and others like him, become valiant servants of the Lord.

The Holy Spirit guided me every step of the way with this book. For example, the idea for Part III came through revelation three years ago as my family was reading the Book of Mormon together.

I truly hope that everyone who reads my book will be uplifted, changed, and motivated to valiantly serve in God's army and stand for truth and righteousness no matter the cost.

PART I: The War Story

CHAPTER 1
The Heroes, the Villains, and the Deceived

The war chapters of the Book of Mormon are filled with stories about heroes and villains who had vastly different reasons for fighting and vastly different ways in which they prepared to fight. The heroes of these chapters were not all Nephites, but they fought for the Nephite cause. Let's learn about these *heroic* groups of people.

Heroic Groups

The Nephites: Their desire was to support their lands, homes, and families, protecting them from their enemies. They also wanted to keep their rights and liberties so they could worship God as they wished. The Nephites knew the Lamanites hated them and would kill them and the people of Ammon if they fell into their hands, so the Nephites protected the people of Ammon the best they could. They had been taught to defend themselves against their enemies if they needed to, but to never start the fighting, and to never shed blood unless they were defending their lives. They believed that if they kept the commandments, God would help them in their battles by warning them of danger or preparing them for war. They knew He would deliver them if they were faithful and resisted sin (Alma 43:9-12; Alma 48:14-16).

The People of Ammon: Also known as the Anti-Nephi-Lehies, these people were once Lamanites who were converted to the Lord by the teachings of Ammon and his brethren. They felt so horrible about shedding so much innocent blood, they made a sign of repentance to the Lord by burying all their weapons of war and making an oath to never stain their swords again. The Nephites gave refuge to these converts in the land of Jershon, protecting them for years from the cruelty of the wicked Lamanites. When Alma and his brethren taught and converted the poor of the Zoramites, the wicked Zoramites kicked them out of their lands. The outcasts then came to Jershon, and the people of Ammon took care of them. They refused to listen to the command of the wicked Zoramites to cast those poor souls out from among them. This angered the wicked Zoramites, who then joined the Lamanites to go to war against the Nephites. In response, the people of Ammon took the poor Zoramites to Melek and gave their land of Jershon to the Nephite armies so they could prepare for battle (Alma 24:6-19; Alma 27-28; Alma 35; Alma 43:11-13).

The Stripling Warriors: Stripling means young, and was a word often used to describe the sons of the people of Ammon. When they saw that their fathers wanted to fight alongside the Nephites, but couldn't due to their oath, they decided to defend the land in their fathers' places. They covenanted to fight for Nephite liberty and to even lay down their lives for it so they could protect themselves and their brethren from bondage. They asked the prophet Helaman to be their leader. Though they were young, they were valiant, courageous, strong, and active. They made sure they were always true and trustworthy. They were men of truth and soberness. Their parents had taught them to always keep God's commandments and walk in His ways. They especially found strength from their faithful mothers who taught them that if they did not doubt, God would deliver them (Alma 53:16-21; Alma 56:47-48). *Fun fact: even though we always call them the stripling warriors, they were never referred to as such in the Book of Mormon. At different times they were called stripling soldiers, stripling sons, and stripling Ammonites.*

The Freemen: They honored their chief judge, Pahoran, and wished to maintain the rights and privileges of religion by a free government (Alma 51:6-7).

****

The *villainous* groups of the war chapters were not all Lamanites, but they all fought against the Nephite cause of freedom and thirsted for power. Let's learn about the two major *villainous* groups.

Villainous Groups

The Lamanites: These people had a centuries-long hatred toward the Nephites. When the wicked Amalekites and Zoramites (apostate Nephite groups) joined their armies, it wasn't hard to stir them up to anger against the Nephites. They wanted to bring the Nephites into bondage so they could make a kingdom over all the land. They willingly fought like dragons to defeat the Nephites and take away their liberty (Alma 43:7-8, 29, 44).

The King-men: As men of noble birth who wanted to be kings, they did not like having chief judges and free government. People like them, who also sought power and authority over others, supported their cause. They refused to fight for the cause of liberty — why must they? In fact, they would rather rebel against their leaders and take over (Alma 51:5, 8, 13; Alma 61:3-5).

****

Now that we know who the groups are, let's look at the *individuals* of the war chapters that exhilarate and infuriate us:

The Heroes

Alma: As high priest of the church, Alma led a mission into Nephite lands, bringing many to repentance. As a result of preaching and ministering in Antionum, the poor of the Zoramite people were filled with joy and peace as they learned they could pray anytime and anywhere. The wicked Zoramites were filled with anger at this ministering, starting a series of events that led to the beginning of the war. This brought Alma much sorrow. The next year, Alma blessed his sons and the church on condition of faithfulness. He then left Zarahemla and was never heard of again. He was a righteous man, thought to have been taken up by the Spirit, like Moses (Alma 31-35; Alma 45:1-19).

Captain Moroni: When he was only 25 years old, Moroni was appointed to be the chief captain of the entire Nephite army. The Prophet Mormon would later describe him as a strong and mighty man who had perfect understanding, did not like shedding blood, and found joy in the liberty and freedom of his country. His heart was filled with thankfulness to God for blessing his people. Moroni worked tirelessly for his people's well-being and safety. He had a firm faith in Christ, and promised to always defend his people, rights, country, and religion, even if he had to die to do it. Moroni had faith that God would tell the Nephites where to go to defend themselves against their enemies and would deliver them from their hands. He gloried in doing good, protecting his people, keeping the commandments, and resisting sin. Mormon said that if all men had been and could be like Moroni, that the devil would never have power over the hearts of the children of men. No more honorable words could be spoken of any person. Mormon called Moroni a man of God just like the sons of Mosiah and Alma and his sons. Moroni did not seek glory or power for himself — only the glory of God and the freedom and welfare of his country (Alma 43:16-17; Alma 48:11-18, Alma 60:36).

Lehi: As a Nephite chief captain, Lehi fought with Moroni in most of his battles. Moroni was his beloved friend, whose safety always brought him to rejoicing. Lehi was like him in faithfulness and devotion to liberty. The Lamanites greatly feared Lehi, perhaps because he greatly loved his people and the cause of liberty and would do anything to protect them. Lehi was grateful for the love he received from his fellow Nephites (Alma 49:17; Alma 53:2).

Helaman: As Alma the Younger's eldest son, Helaman and his brothers, Shiblon and Corianton, faithfully preached the gospel of repentance to all the Nephite lands. They baptized all those who would follow their words. The prophet Mormon said that Helaman and his brothers were no less serviceable than beloved Captain Moroni because their efforts were just as important to the well-being of the Nephites. When Helaman's father, Alma, left Zarahemla, Helaman became the prophet. In the 11th year of the war, the young sons of the people of Ammon asked him to be their leader as they decided to fight alongside the Nephites. He loved those stripling warriors like his own sons. Helaman had so much gratitude to God for His mercy, and he strove to serve his fellow chief captains and armies to the best of his ability. He genuinely cared for and loved his brethren (Alma 43:1-2; Alma 48:19; Alma 53:19-22).

Morianton's Maid Servant: After being abused by Morianton, his maid servant fled to Captain Moroni's camp to provide crucial information regarding Morianton's plans to flee (Alma 50:30-31).

Teancum: Along with his brothers in Christ, Moroni and Lehi, Teancum was a Nephite chief captain, revered by many as a mighty and great warrior. His men were all stronger and more skilled in war than even the Lamanites. He always strove to fight valiantly for his country as a loyal friend to liberty. No manner of afflictions could change his devotion to fighting for freedom (Alma 51:31; Alma 62:37).

Pahoran: The son of Nephihah, and the third Nephite chief judge in the Book of Mormon. Pahoran strove to be a righteous man. He did not seek glory, but rather the freedom of his people and country. He made a sacred oath to judge righteously and to keep the peace and freedom of the people. He promised to grant them the privilege of worshiping God, and to maintain the cause of God, as well as bring the wicked to justice. Again, he did not seek power, but simply to preserve the rights and liberty of his people (Alma 50:39; Alma 61:9).

Laman: After the Lamanite king was killed by Amalickiah, Laman, one of the king's servants, ran away with the other servants and joined the people of Ammon. Amalickiah falsely blamed Laman and his brethren for killing the king. In the 12th year of the war, he and a few others bravely faced the Lamanites by pretending to be Lamanites to help free Nephite prisoners of war (Alma 47:25-29; Alma 55).

Antipus: The Nephite captain in Judea, Antipus strove to be a valiant and determined leader. He and his army worked tirelessly to fortify and protect their city. They were determined to conquer or die (Alma 56:9, 15-17).

Gid: A Nephite chief captain, Gid was a faithful follower of Christ, and he knew that God delivered his people. He led the band taking the Lamanite prisoners to Zarahemla, and he also worked strategically with chief captains Teomner and Lehi to take back the city of Manti without battling the Lamanites (Alma 57:28-35; Alma 58:1-28).

Teomner: He worked strategically with chief captains Gid and Lehi to take back the city of Manti without battling the Lamanites (Alma 58:1-28).

The Villains

Zerahemnah: Zerahemnah was the appointed chief commander of the Lamanites who quickly stirred them up to anger against the Nephites and the people of Ammon. He started a war with them and appointed the Amalekites and Zoramites (apostate Nephite groups) as chief captains. They found more pleasure in killing than the Lamanites did and could inspire them to fight like dragons. Zerahemnah couldn't wait to gain power over the Nephites and take away their freedoms. He led the first battle against the Nephites in the long war (Alma 43-44).

Amalickiah: Described as a large, strong, and wealthy man, Amalickiah was a Nephite who loathed Helaman's teachings so much, he wanted to kill him and his brethren. He wanted nothing more than to be a mighty king who would destroy the church of God and religious liberty. He didn't care how many would have to die to make that happen. He loved to use flattery and cunning to lead others to do wickedness. He could do evil in the subtlest of ways, tricking many. He didn't really care about those who followed him – he just wanted to gain power over the whole land (Alma 46:3-4, 10; Alma 47:4; Alma 49:10).

Morianton: Morianton was a contentious and greedy man with a passionate temper who hated negotiating. He was so stubborn he would much rather fight than talk and settle things peacefully. He was excellent at using flattering words to inspire his people to battle (Alma 50:25-35).

Ammoron: As Amalickiah's brother, he became the Lamanite king after Teancum slew him. He hated the Nephites as much as his brother did and loved shedding blood for his wicked purposes. Captain Moroni called him a child of hell (Alma 52:3; Alma 54:11).

Jacob the Zoramite: A man who fought with great fury and an unconquerable spirit, Jacob the Zoramite was the leader of the Lamanites in the land of Mulek.

He was determined to slay the Nephites even if the odds weren't in his favor (Alma 52:33-34).

Pachus: The king of the king-men, Pachus and the king-men drove the freemen out of Zarahemla, threw Pahoran off his judgment-seat, and took possession of the land. He couldn't care less about sending support and provisions to Helaman or anyone else fighting in the war (Alma 62:6).

The Deceived

King of the Lamanites: Being stirred up to anger by Amalickiah, the Lamanite king sent a proclamation throughout his lands requiring the Lamanites to gather and go to battle against the Nephites. He was angry when many of them were too afraid to fight, so he hired Amalickiah to coerce them into battle. Little did he know Amalickiah had a plan to dethrone him (Alma 47:1, 3, 21-24).

Lehonti: Many of the Lamanites were too afraid to fight the Nephites, and Lehonti was appointed to be their king. After finally giving in to Amalickiah's constant request for him to come off the mount, he realized too late after trusting him that that was a mistake (Alma 47:6, 10-14, 18).

Queen of the Lamanites: Upon hearing the news of her husband's murder, the Lamanite queen pleaded with Amalickiah to spare her people and to testify concerning the tragedy. Tricked by Amalickiah (and his servants), she became his wife (Alma 47:32-35).

****

Now that we know why the war between the Nephites and Lamanites started, and we know all about the heroes and villains (and those they deceived), let's talk about each year of the war and what we can learn from it. The war lasted off and on for almost 14 years, with some years of peace in between. That's a lot of fighting.

It's time to get out your scriptures and a writing utensil to start studying and journaling. This is going to be life-changing!

CHAPTER 2
Year 1 of the War Chapters

Alma 43

While Alma and his sons preached the gospel among the Nephites, the Zoramites joined the Lamanites and prepared for war. When the Nephites saw that the Lamanites were preparing for war against them, they prepared as well and gathered at the land of Jershon. The Lamanites gathered at the land of Antionum. Their leader, Zerahemnah, appointed Amalekites and Zoramites to be chief captains over them since they were even more wicked and murderous than the Lamanites. The descendants of the Nephite dissenters were almost as numerous as the Nephites themselves! Hatred was the key to Zerahemnah's strategy in bringing the Nephites into bondage.

Captain Moroni met the Lamanites in the borders of the Land of Jershon. The Nephites were heavily armed with weapons of war and wore thick clothing and protective armor. The Lamanites, while also armed with weapons, only wore loincloths (the Amalekites and Zoramites did have more clothing). Even though there were twice as many Lamanites, they were afraid of the Nephites due to their great armor of breastplates and shields.

The Lamanites didn't want to fight Moroni's army. Instead of meeting them in Jershon, they ran into the wilderness hoping to overtake the land of Manti. Moroni sent spies to watch the Lamanites, and sent men to ask Alma, the prophet, to pray to find out where they must go to defend themselves. The Lord informed Alma that the Lamanites were heading through the wilderness to Manti to attack the weaker part of the people.

President Spencer W. Kimball taught the importance of listening to the prophet's voice: *"Let us hearken to those we sustain as prophets and seers, as well as the other brethren as if our eternal life depended upon it, because it does!" (Conference Report, Apr. 1978, 117; or Ensign, May 1978, 77)*

When Moroni got this prophecy from Alma, he left some of his army in Jershon to protect it, and then took the rest to Manti. He called the people of that part of the land to join in the battle against the Lamanites so they could defend their lands, rights, and liberties.

Moroni and his army hid in the valley near the bank of the west side of the river Sidon, and had spies watch for the Lamanites to arrive. He split his army into two parts, and had them hide, making them ready to meet the Lamanites. Moroni had command of one part, and chief captain Lehi had command of the other.

When the Lamanites started to cross the river, Lehi's army surrounded them and started to fight. Many more Lamanites than Nephites were dying due to their lack of armor, and the Lamanites started to get scared.

Let's think of armor spiritually, like with the metaphor of the armor of God. President Harold B. Lee explained about wearing the whole armor of God:

> "We have the four parts of the body that the Apostle Paul said or saw to be the most vulnerable to the powers of darkness. The loins, typifying virtue, chastity. The heart typifying our conduct. Our feet, our goals or objectives in life and finally our head, our thoughts.
>
> "… We should have our loins girt about with truth. What is truth? Truth, the Lord said, was knowledge of things as they are, things as they were and things as they are to come [D&C 93:24]. … 'Our loins shall be girt about with truth,' the prophet said.
>
> "And the heart, what kind of a breastplate shall protect our conduct in life? We shall have over our hearts a breastplate of righteousness. Well, having learned truth we have a measure by which we can judge between right and wrong and so our conduct will always be gauged by that thing which we know to be true. Our breastplate to cover our conduct shall be the breastplate of righteousness.
>
> "[By] what shall we protect our feet, or by what shall we gauge our objectives or our goals in

life? ... 'Your feet should be shod with the preparation of the gospel of peace.' (Ephesians 6:15). ...

"And then finally the helmet of salvation. ... What is salvation? Salvation is to be saved. Saved from what? Saved from death and saved from sin. ...

"Well, now the Apostle Paul ... had his armoured man holding in his hand a shield and in his other hand a sword, which were the weapons of those days. That shield was the shield of faith, and the sword was the sword of the spirit which is the Word of God. I can't think of any more powerful weapons than faith and a knowledge of the scriptures in the which are contained the Word of God. One so armoured and one so prepared with those weapons is prepared to go out against the enemy." (Feet Shod with the Preparation of the Gospel of Peace, Brigham Young University Speeches of the Year [Nov. 9, 1954], 2–3, 6–7; see also Ephesians 6:13–17; D&C 27:15–18)

REFLECTION: *Just like the Nephite army was protected by their physical armor, how are you protected as you wear the whole armor of God?*

The Lamanites ran toward the river, with Lehi's army chasing them. They crossed the river but Lehi's army stayed on the bank so they couldn't turn back, while Moroni's army met them on the other side and started to kill them. No matter where the Lamanites went, they were met by Nephites. But the Lamanites, instead of running away, were inspired by their Amalekite and Zoramite captains, and began to fight like dragons, with more courage and anger than they ever had before. In their intense anger, they pierced through armor and cut off many arms.

The Nephites knew they were fighting for a better cause than the Lamanites (they were fighting for their families, freedoms, and faith rather than for power and removal of other's liberties), but because of the fierceness and anger of the Lamanites, they were afraid and almost ran from them.

> *REFLECTION: What do you think are worthy causes for war (see Alma 43:30)? You may never fight in a war in your life, but you may have to fight in some metaphorical wars, perhaps with coworkers, family, companies, etc. How would you know if your cause was just?*

President Gordon B. Hinckley offered some light on this subject:

"… We are a freedom-loving people, committed to the defense of liberty wherever it is in jeopardy. I believe that God will not hold men and women in uniform responsible as agents of their government in carrying forward that which they are legally obligated to do. It may even be that He will hold us responsible if we try to impede or hedge up the way of those who are involved in a contest with forces of evil and repression." (in Conference Report, Apr. 2003, 83–84; or Ensign, May 2003, 80)

Moroni inspired his men with thoughts of why they were defending themselves, persuading them to stand their ground rather than run. They prayed together in one voice for strength from God. The Nephites were filled with so much power that at the same hour they prayed, the Lamanites started running from them toward the river Sidon. *What a perfect example of how sincere prayer works!*

There were more than double the number of Lamanites than Nephites, but they had been driven so much that they were surrounded on both sides of the river by Moroni's and Lehi's men. The Lamanites were terrified. When Moroni saw their fear, instead of finishing them off, he commanded that his men stop killing them.

> **REFLECTION: Why didn't Moroni just kill them when he had the chance? What Christlike qualities did he have to help him stop killing? How can you use those same qualities in your life?**

Alma 44

Moroni's men stopped killing the Lamanites and stepped back. Moroni explained to Zerahemnah that he and the Nephites were not men of blood and didn't want to slay them even though they easily could. They didn't want power over the Lamanites or to bring them into bondage, but that was *exactly* what the Lamanites wanted. Moroni called them out and said the Lamanites were only angry with them because of their religion.

> *REFLECTION: Why do people get angry about another's religion? How can you prevent yourself and others from feeling that way?*

Moroni bore his testimony saying that the Lord was with the Nephites and had delivered the Lamanites into their hands due to their religion and faith in Christ. The Lamanites could NOT destroy their faith. Moroni proclaimed that God would support, keep, and preserve the Nephites if they were faithful. Only if they fell into transgression and denied their faith would the Lord let them be destroyed.

Moroni then commanded Zerahemnah and his men, in the name of God who had strengthened them, (listing all the reasons why the Nephites had gained that power over them), to lay down their weapons so they could keep their lives.

> *REFLECTION: Read the reasons Moroni gave in Alma 44:5. He said that the Nephites owed all their happiness to the sacred word of God. What do you think he meant by that? How have you seen that in your life?*

If the Lamanites would put their weapons down and end the war, they would be spared, but if not, Moroni would command his men *to inflict the wounds of death* that they *may become extinct (Vs. 7).* Then they would see who had power and who would be brought into bondage!

Zerahemnah partially complied by handing Moroni his sword, cimeter, and bow. But he would not make an oath that he knew the Lamanites and their children would never keep. He asked that the Nephites take their weapons and let them go into the wilderness. If not, they would continue to fight, either dying or conquering.

The Lamanites did not believe in God and did not believe He had any part in delivering the Lamanites into the Nephites' hands. Zerahemnah said that it was the Nephites' cunning and armor that had preserved them so far.

REFLECTION: Have you ever failed to recognize God's hand in your life? How have you since come to recognize it?

Captain Moroni, unwilling to take back what he said, returned the weapons to Zerahemnah, saying, *Behold, we will end the conflict (Vs. 10)*. He boldly repeated his terms: if the Lamanites would not agree, their blood would be spilt.

This made Zerahemnah angry. He rushed to kill Captain Moroni, but as he did, one of Moroni's soldiers ran to his aid. He knocked Zerahemnah's sword to the ground, breaking it, and then cut off Zerahemnah's scalp. Zerahemnah, scared and wounded, backed away and joined his soldiers.

The Nephite soldier who took off the scalp, lifted it up by the hair onto the point of his sword and stretched it forth so everyone could see it. Loudly he prophesied, *Even as this scalp has fallen to the earth, which is the scalp of your chief, so shall ye fall to the earth except ye will deliver up your weapons of war and depart with a covenant of peace (Vs. 14)*.

Many of the Lamanites were scared and did as they were commanded, and then were free to go into the wilderness in peace.

However, Zerahemnah was furious, which made the rest of his soldiers angry, inspiring them to fight with even more power.

Moroni was angry too, because of the stubbornness of the Lamanites, and commanded his army to start killing them again. The Lamanites fought with all their might, but as they did, their nakedness caused them to fall quickly, fulfilling the prophecy of the Nephite soldier.

Zerahemnah, when he finally realized that they were going to all be destroyed, begged Captain Moroni to spare them if they would make the covenant of peace and never go to war against the Nephites again. Moroni, as promised, stopped the fighting, took the Lamanites' weapons, and let them leave after they made the covenant.

There were so many deaths on both sides that they could not be numbered. The dead were cast into the waters of Sidon, burying them deep in the sea. The Nephite armies who were left returned home.

> *REFLECTION: Based on this first story, what is your overall impression of Zerahemnah? List the qualities he showed. Consider how, if he had the opposite qualities, this story may have changed.*

> *REFLECTION: What did you learn about Moroni from this first battle? See these verses in Alma for help: 43:19, 23, 30, 54; 44:11, 20.*

CHAPTER 3
Year 2 of The War Chapters

Alma 45

The Nephites were so grateful that the Lord had delivered them out of the hands of their enemies. They fasted, prayed, and worshiped God with joy.

Back in Zarahemla, Alma spoke to his son, Helaman, about his testimony of Christ and the importance of keeping His commandments. He blessed his son to be prosperous and then confided in him that four hundred years after Christ would come to visit their posterity, the Lord would allow the Lamanites to destroy the Nephites from off the face of the earth due to their unbelief and works of darkness. After this prophecy, Alma blessed

Helaman, his brothers, the Nephite lands, and the church, so long as they would be faithful. Alma then left Zarahemla, never to be seen again.

Elder Bruce R. McConkie explained that the phrase *"taken up by the Spirit, or buried by the hand of the Lord" (Alma 45:19) suggests that Alma was translated: "Moses, Elijah, and Alma the younger, were translated" (Mormon Doctrine, 2nd ed. [1966], 805).*

After his father left, Helaman and his brethren declared the gospel and established the church again in every Nephite city, appointing priests and teachers. There were many prideful Nephites who would not listen to them because they loved their riches and didn't want to keep the commandments.

> *REFLECTION: See Alma 45:24. How could being "rich in their own eyes" affect a person's receptiveness to gospel teachings and keep them from "walking uprightly before God?"*

Alma 46

Some of these Nephite dissenters were so angry, they wanted to kill Helaman and his brethren. The leader of these men was a large and strong man named Amalickiah who wanted to be a king. He promised his followers that if they supported him, he would make them rulers over the people. Even some high priests believed his flattery and left the church. Amalickiah, as king, wanted to destroy the church of God and abolish religious liberty.

> *REFLECTION: See Alma 46:8-10. If "the children of men" can so quickly forget their Lord, how can you be sure you don't? How can you ensure you don't listen to wicked people, ideas, and sources?*

President George Albert Smith taught, *"If you cross to the devil's side of the line one inch, you are in the tempter's power, and if he is successful, you will not be able to think or even reason properly, because you will have lost the spirit of the Lord"* (George Albert Smith, *Teachings of Presidents of the Church: George Albert Smith, Chapter 18*).

When Captain Moroni heard of Amalickiah and his followers, he was terribly angry, and tore a piece of his coat off, writing: *In memory of our God, our religion, and freedom, and our peace, our wives, and our children (Vs. 12).* He attached the cloth to the end of a pole, put on his armor, and bowed down and prayed to God for liberty for the Christians, on condition of their righteousness.

> *REFLECTION: See Alma 46:15. Christians are true believers of Christ and faithful members of His church. How can you, like the righteous Nephites, gladly take upon yourself His name?*

Moroni prayed for his fellow Christians with faith that God would only allow their destruction due to wickedness. He also prayed for the freedom of the *land of liberty (Vs. 17)*. After this humble prayer, Moroni went to the Nephite people, waving his flag, and crying for them to make a covenant for the cause of liberty. They ran to do so, and covenanted to keep the commandments, else they would lose their freedom or lives.

The Nephites showed their devotion to the covenant by ripping their clothing. They knew that if they fell into transgression and were ashamed to take the name of Christ upon them, that the Lord would rip them as they had ripped their clothing. They cast their clothing down at Moroni's feet, making a covenant that God would allow their enemies to destroy them if they fell into sin.

Elder Paul E. Koelliker counseled:

> *"Giving careful attention to covenant making is critical to our eternal salvation. Covenants are agreements we make with our Heavenly Father in which we commit our hearts, minds, and behavior to keeping the commandments defined by the Lord. As we are faithful in keeping our agreement, He covenants, or promises, to bless us, ultimately with all that He has." ("Gospel Covenants Bring Promised Blessings," Ensign or Liahona, Nov. 2005, 94)*

REFLECTION: What blessings have you received from making and keeping covenants?

Moroni reminded those who had made the covenant that they were descendants of Joseph of Egypt. Just as part of Joseph's coat was preserved, the Nephites would be preserved if they had faith in Christ. Moroni gathered people from all the Nephite lands to covenant for the cause of liberty.

President Joseph Fielding Smith taught:

> *"We are told that there was a prophecy in the destruction of the coat of many colors worn by Joseph. Part of it was preserved, and Jacob, before his death, prophesied that as a remnant of the coat was preserved so should a remnant of Joseph's posterity be preserved [see Alma 46:24].*
>
> *"That remnant now found among the Lamanites shall eventually partake of the blessings of the Gospel. They shall unite with the remnant which is being gathered from among the nations and they shall be blessed of the Lord forever." (The Way to Perfection [1970], 121)*

Amalickiah realized, with fear, that there were so many more men in Captain Moroni's army than in his. Knowing his cause to be weak, he fled with whoever would go with him into the land of Nephi. Many of his people would not go, because they were doubtful of their cause and were afraid.

> *REFLECTION: See Alma 46:29. What is the importance of the cause when following someone? Think of Joseph Smith and the early Saints. Most of them remained faithful when it would have been easy to abandon their cause.*

Captain Moroni knew that it would be dangerous if Amalickiah joined the Lamanites, so he took his armies and cut off Amalickiah's people as they fled. Most of them were taken prisoner, while only Amalickiah and a few of his men escaped. Moroni commanded the prisoners to make an oath of peace or be put to death. Most chose peace.

The Title of Liberty was then hoisted upon every Nephite tower, so the standard of liberty would be planted among the Nephites.

> **REFLECTION: What standards should you plant in your heart to help you be a faithful follower of Christ?**

Peace was once again established in the lands of the Nephites, and Helaman and the high priests maintained order in the church. There was much rejoicing (even concerning those that lost their lives), and the people were firm in their faith in Christ.

> *REFLECTION: In Alma 46:40 it says that God had prepared many plants and roots to remove the cause of diseases. Think of and write down other remedies that God has prepared over time to help with sickness and ponder on the mercy of a loving God.*

Alma 47

While there was peace among the Nephites during this time, Amalickiah was busy plotting. Amalickiah and his followers made it to the land of Nephi. They stirred up the Lamanites to anger against the Nephites. The Lamanite king then sent a proclamation, commanding the people to prepare for war. Many were afraid and didn't want to fight because they didn't want to die.

Even though they feared displeasing the king, most of the Lamanites did not obey the king's command. The king was angry because of their disobedience, so he sent Amalickiah with his army to compel those Lamanites to fight. Amalickiah was happy about this arrangement because he secretly wanted to become king of the Lamanites, and he had a plan to do so.

> *REFLECTION: Alma 47:4 says that Amalickiah was a "very subtle man to do evil." This means that he came across as good and agreeable, but in reality, he had wicked schemes to hurt others and build himself up. How can you recognize when someone has selfish and bad intentions?*

Amalickiah had already gotten the favor of the obedient Lamanites, and now wanted to get the favor of the disobedient ones. He went to Onidah (the place of arms), where the Lamanite dissenters had fled. They had appointed a king (Lehonti) and were determined not to fight the Nephites. Lehonti's followers had gone to the top of Mount Antipas to prepare to fight Amalickiah's army, but Amalickiah had no intention of fighting them because he wanted their favor to further his purposes.

He told his army to pitch their tents in the valley near Antipas. That night, Amalickiah sent a secret embassy into Mount Antipas, asking King Lehonti to come down to the foot of the mount to speak with him. Lehonti would not do it. Amalickiah asked again and Lehonti still wouldn't do it. He asked a third time. When Amalickiah found he couldn't get Lehonti to come down, he went up the mount, almost to Lehonti's camp, and sent a fourth time, saying if Lehonti came down, he could bring his guards with him. Lehonti finally did so.

> *REFLECTION: How does Satan try to get you to come down from higher ground? Think about how he tempts you to lower your standards, saying everything will be fine and no harm will be done.*

Amalickiah told Lehonti to come with his army at night and surround Amalickiah's men. The deal was that Amalickiah would deliver those men into Lehonti's hands if he would make Amalickiah a second leader over the army. Lehonti agreed and followed Amalickiah's plan.

> **REFLECTION: Why do you think Lehonti finally trusted and listened to Amalickiah? Have you ever done something similar?**

Amalickiah's men, seeing they were surrounded, didn't want to be destroyed, so they pleaded to fall in with Lehonti's men. Amalickiah wanted this to happen so he could dethrone Lehonti. He knew that if the Lamanites' chief leader were killed, the second leader would be promoted, and he was that second leader. So, Amalickiah had one of his servants give Lehonti poison *by degrees*, or slowly, until he died *(Vs. 18)*.

Sister Elaine S. Dalton said,

> *"Could it be that this may be happening today? Could it be that first we tolerate, then accept, and eventually embrace the vice that surrounds us? Could it be that we have been deceived by false role models and persuasive media messages that cause us to forget our divine identity? Are we too being poisoned by degrees? What could be more deceptive than to entice the youth of this noble generation to do nothing or to be busy ever-texting but never coming to a knowledge of the truths contained in a book that was written for you and your day by prophets of God — the Book of Mormon? What could be more deceptive than to entice women, young and old, you and me, to be so involved in ourselves, our looks, our clothes, our body shape and size that we lose sight of our divine identity and our ability to change the world through our virtuous influence? What could be more deceptive than to entice men — young and old, holding the holy priesthood of God — to view seductive pornography and thus focus on flesh instead of faith, to be consumers of vice rather than guardians of virtue? The Book of Mormon relates the story of 2,000 young heroes*

whose virtue and purity gave them the strength to defend their parents' covenants and their family's faith. Their virtue and commitment to be 'true at all times' changed the world!" ("A Return to Virtue," General Conference October 2008)

REFLECTION: How does Satan seek to poison you "by degrees?" What would the poison represent spiritually? See Sister Dalton's quote above for help.

Elder Robert D. Hales taught,

"Some may try to provoke us and engage us in argument. In the Book of Mormon, we read about Lehonti and his men camped upon a mount. The traitorous Amalickiah urged Lehonti to 'come

down' and meet him in the valley. But when Lehonti left the high ground, he was poisoned 'by degrees' until he died, and his army fell into Amalickiah's hands (see Alma 47). By arguments and accusations, some people bait us to leave the high ground. The high ground is where the light is. It's where we see the first light of morning and the last light in the evening. It is the safe ground. It is true and where knowledge is. Sometimes others want us to come down off the high ground and join them in a theological scrum in the mud. These few contentious individuals are set on picking religious fights, online or in person. We are always better staying on the higher ground of mutual respect and love." ("Christian Courage: The Price of Discipleship," Ensign or Liahona, Nov. 2008, 74)

With Lehonti dead, Amalickiah became the leader and chief commander of the Lamanites. The first order of business was to return to Nephi, the chief Lamanite city. The Lamanite king came out with his guards to meet Amalickiah, thinking he had done what he had commanded him to do. Amalickiah sent his servants to the king. His servants bowed down, pretending to revere the king, and then as the king put out his hand to raise them up peacefully, one of them stabbed him in the heart.

The servants of the king ran away in fear, and Amalickiah's servants blamed the king's servants for the murder. Amalickiah himself wasn't there to make the accusation so that he could make his next deceitful move.

> *REFLECTION: What harm do false accusations do? Knowing that false accusations happen, how can you be more sensitive to what is actually true?*

Amalickiah, "hearing about" the king's murder, pretended to be angry and had a search done for the servants. The servants, who were afraid for their lives, had run into the wilderness and joined the people of Ammon in Zarahemla. They were thankfully not found by Amalickiah's men.

> *REFLECTION: Alma 47:30 says that "by his fraud," [Amalickiah] gained the hearts of the people." There may be people who pretend to care about you but really just want to see you fall. How can you ensure the people in your life are sincere and genuinely want what's best for you?*

The next day, Amalickiah with his armies took possession of the city of Nephi. After the queen had found out what had happened to her husband (Amalickiah had sent an embassy to inform her), she asked him to spare her city and to come see her, bringing witnesses to testify of her husband's death. The same servants who killed the king were the "witnesses" against the kings' servants, and the queen believed their story. *How twisted!*

> **REFLECTION: *This story teaches so many lessons, and one is that false accusations happen. Not everything is as it seems. Nobody should be quick to accuse and judge others. Do you have any thoughts from these lessons? Can you think of any more lessons from this story?***

Amalickiah sought the queen's favor, and then married her. Through his *fraud and cunning servants*, Amalickiah became the king of all the Lamanites, which included many groups of people, including Nephite dissenters (Vs. 35). These Nephite dissenters became more *hardened, impenitent, wild, wicked,* and *ferocious* than the Lamanites (Vs. 36). They had completely forgotten the Lord.

REFLECTION: Why do you think that those who started out with the truth of Christ would be so much more wicked than those who never had the truth?

Elder Neal A. Maxwell said,

"There are the dissenters who leave the Church, either formally or informally, but who cannot leave it alone. Usually anxious to please worldly galleries, they are critical or at least condescending towards the Brethren. They not only seek to steady the ark but also on occasion

give it a hard shove! Often having been taught the same true doctrines as the faithful, they have nevertheless moved in the direction of dissent (see Alma 47:36). They have minds hardened by pride (see Daniel 5:20)." (Men and Women of Christ [1991], 4)

Elder Russell M. Nelson taught,

"'He that hath the spirit of contention is not of me [saith the Lord]' ... (3 Nephi 11:29–30). Throughout the world, Saints of the Lord ... have learned that the path of dissent leads to real dangers. How divisive is the force of dissension! Small acts can lead to such great consequences. Regardless of position or situation, no one can safely assume immunity to contention's terrible toll. 'Contention fosters disunity.' (Conference Report, Apr. 1989, 86–88; or Ensign, May 1989, 68, 70)

Alma 48

After Amalickiah became the king of all the Lamanites, he didn't stop there — no, he wanted to rule over all the Lamanite and Nephite lands! Near the end of that year, he turned the Lamanites' hearts against the Nephites, and appointed men to speak on their towers against them. Amalickiah indeed hardened the Lamanites' hearts and blinded their minds, stirring them up to anger and gathering a large enough army to battle the Nephites. He was absolutely determined to bring the Nephites into bondage. So, he appointed Zoramites to be the chief captains because they were the most familiar with

Nephite strengths and weaknesses. They started toward Zarahemla.

Meanwhile, Moroni was helping his people remain faithful to the Lord, as well as strengthening his armies and fortifications. He put the most men in the weakest fortifications to best protect the Nephite lands. His cause was to support what his enemies called the *cause of Christians* (Vs. 10).

Alma 49

In the last month of the year, on the tenth day, the Lamanites approached the city of Ammonihah, thinking it would be easy to take over since they had once destroyed it. When they arrived, they were shocked at the fortifications Moroni had built! He had stationed an army by the borders of the land and had cast up dirt about the land to shield them from the Lamanites' stones and arrows. The dirt was so high, the Lamanites could only attack from the city's entrance.

REFLECTION: Read Alma 49:7 to find out what the Lamanites were fighting for. How did that contrast with the Nephites? See Alma 46:12-16.

The Lamanite chief captains were astonished at the Nephites' wisdom. Even though the Lamanites had prepared themselves with a great army and wore thick, protective armor, they no longer believed they could easily defeat the Nephites after seeing their level of preparedness — a preparedness they had never seen among the Nephites until that moment!

> *REFLECTION: Just as the Lamanites had gotten stronger over time, requiring that the Nephites better prepare for their attacks, in these last days it's so important to be better prepared for Satan's attacks. What more can you do to resist Satan's temptations?*

Since Amalickiah wasn't there to force his army to fight the Nephites, the chief captains decided to retreat into the wilderness.

President James E. Faust taught, *"Satan is our greatest enemy and works night and day to destroy us. But we need not become paralyzed with fear of Satan's power. He can have no power over us unless we permit it. He is really a coward, and if we stand firm he will retreat"* ("Be Not Afraid," Ensign, Oct. 2002, 4).

The Lamanites then marched to the land of Noah, thinking it would be the next easiest place to conquer. The chief captains were determined to conquer, and even made an oath they would destroy the people of that city. To their surprise, the city of Noah was no longer weak, but strong — even stronger than the city Ammonihah, all thanks to Moroni's fortifications! Moroni figured this would happen — that the Lamanites would be scared when arriving at Ammonihah and would then go to Noah thinking it was the weakest land. What wisdom he had! He even appointed Lehi, a man the Lamanites greatly feared, as the chief captain in the city of Noah.

REFLECTION: Moroni strengthened his weaker cities, surprising the Lamanites and preventing them from conquering those lands. Read Ether 12:27 and ponder how Christ can help make your weaknesses into strengths. Write down weaknesses you wish to overcome. Pray for help.

Despite the city's strength, since the Lamanite chief captains had already made an oath to attack, they had to go through with it. Now, just like at Ammonihah, the Lamanites could only infiltrate the forts through the entrance due to the high banks and deep ditches surrounding the city. The Nephites were prepared to destroy everyone who tried to enter the fort outside the entrance with stones and arrows. They were also prepared with the strongest men carrying swords and slings to kill all who would come into their place of security through the entrance. The Nephites were prepared on all sides to defend themselves.

The Lamanites attempted to get into the city through the entrance but were *driven back from time to time* and *slain with an immense slaughter* (Vs. 21). When they realized they couldn't get power there, they tried to dig down the banks. But, instead of being successful, the Nephites threw stones and arrows at them, leaving the Lamanites' dead and wounded bodies to fill up the ditches.

The Nephites clearly had all power over them, but the Lamanites kept attempting to destroy them until their chief captains were all dead. More than one thousand of the Lamanites were killed, but not one of the Nephites fell. Fifty Nephites had been wounded severely in their legs, but their armor and shields had protected them from more life-threatening harm.

REFLECTION: *Think again about the full armor of God and how it can protect us. See Ephesians 6:10-18 for a reminder. *No writing necessary.*

When they realized all their chief captains were slain, the Lamanites returned to the land of Nephi to inform Amalickiah, their king, of their great loss. He was incredibly angry with his people because he had been unable to put the Nephites into bondage. He cursed God and Moroni and swore he would drink his blood — all because Moroni had kept God's commandments and prepared for the safety of his people.

On the other hand, the people of Nephi thanked God for His matchless power in delivering them from their enemies. There was much peace and prosperity in the church because they listened to the words of God declared by Helaman and Ammon and their brethren who had authority to preach repentance and baptize.

Elder Dallin H. Oaks taught, *"The blessings of the gospel are universal, and so is the formula for peace: keep the commandments of God. War and conflict are the result of wickedness; peace is the product of righteousness." ("World Peace," Ensign, May 1990)*

CHAPTER 4
Years 3-6 of The War Chapters

Alma 50:1-16 (Year 3)

Even though the Nephite armies had had much success, Moroni did not stop preparing for war or defending his people against the Lamanites.

Moroni had his armies dig heaps of earth around every Nephite city. On top of the ridges, he had timbers built up to the height of a man, and then upon those timbers he had a frame of pickets built up strong and high.

President Henry B. Eyring taught:

"As the forces around us increase in intensity, whatever spiritual strength was once sufficient will not be enough. And whatever

growth in spiritual strength we once thought was possible, greater growth will be made available to us. Both the need for spiritual strength and the opportunity to acquire it will increase at rates which we underestimate at our peril." ("Always," Ensign, Oct. 1999, 9)

REFLECTION: What can you do to build high spiritual walls against Satan's temptations?

President Ezra Taft Benson counseled, *"It is better to prepare and prevent than it is to repair and repent"* (The Teachings of Ezra Taft Benson [1988], 285).

> **REFLECTION: Why do you think this statement is true? When have you seen an example of the principle this statement teaches?**

Moroni also had towers built to overlook those works of pickets and had places of security on those towers so the Lamanites could not hurt them. From the tower, those guarding could throw stones and other weapons at the Lamanites to stop them from entering the walls of Nephite cities. Strongholds like this were built in every Nephite city in all the land.

REFLECTION: *In a spiritual sense, the watchmen on the tower are the prophets of God. They can see what we cannot from an eternal perspective. If we listen to their warnings, we will be better prepared for future trials, and will be kept safe from our enemy, Satan. Can you think of a prophetic warning that has helped you?*

Elder David A Bednar taught,

"Spiritual complacency and casualness make us vulnerable to the advances of the adversary. Spiritual thoughtlessness invites great danger into our lives...Constant vigilance is required to counteract complacency and

casualness. To be vigilant is the state or action of keeping careful watch for possible danger or difficulties. And keeping watch denotes the act of staying awake to guard and protect. Spiritually speaking, we need to stay awake and be alert to the promptings of the Holy Ghost and the signals that come from the Lord's watchmen on the towers."

He continued, "Understanding the intent of an enemy is vital to effective preparation for possible attacks. Precisely because Captain Moroni knew the intention of the Lamanites, he was prepared to meet them at the time of their coming and was victorious. And that same principle and promise applies to each of us. 'If ye are prepared, ye shall not fear. And that ye might escape the power of the enemy.'" ("Watchful unto Prayer Continually," Ensign, Nov. 2019)

Then Moroni had his armies go into the east wilderness and drive all the Lamanites who were there back into their own lands, south of the land of Zarahemla. Once the Lamanites were gone from that area, Moroni sent those living in and around Zarahemla to possess the land in the east wilderness to the borders by the seashore.

But Moroni wasn't done yet. He also placed armies in the south, in the borders of the Nephite lands, and had them build fortifications to protect their armies and their people from their enemies. By doing so, Moroni cut off all strongholds of the Lamanites in the east and west wilderness, with a strong fortified line between the Nephite and Lamanite lands, the Nephites being on the north and the Lamanites being on the south.

REFLECTION: *Think about and write what you need to "cut off" in your life so you can be holier and protected from Satan's influence.*

Jesus taught,

> *"And if thy right eye offend thee, pluck it out, and cast it from thee: for it is profitable for thee that one of thy members should perish, and not that thy whole body should be cast into hell. And if thy right hand offend thee, cut it off, and cast it from thee: for it is profitable for thee that one of thy members should perish, and not that thy whole body should be cast into hell." (Matthew 5:29–30)*

Captain Moroni was serious about making sure the Lamanites had no power over the Nephite lands or people. Because of his determination and assurance of protection, his armies increased daily.

> **REFLECTION: *You, and all believers in Christ, are a part of God's army. What protection do you receive from Him?***

Was Moroni done? No! He also laid the foundation of new Nephite cities: the city of Moroni by the east sea, and the city of Nephihah, which was between the cities of Moroni and Aaron. Many other cities were being built in the north as well, one being called the city of Lehi, which was on the north side of the east sea.

Alma 50:17-23 (Year 4)

At the beginning of that year, the Nephites were prospering. They were rich and strong and had many children. The Nephites truly felt that the Lord was merciful and just in fulfilling all His words. The Lord had counseled the prophet Lehi hundreds of years earlier that as long as his people were righteous, they would prosper in the land, but if they were wicked, they would be cut off from His presence. In all the time of the Nephites, their wickedness led to wars and destruction, but the faithful were always delivered, while the wicked were put in bondage, killed, dwindled in unbelief, and mingled with the Lamanites.

> *REFLECTION: When have you felt the Lord extend His power and blessings to you for being obedient and for fortifying yourself against temptation?*

> *REFLECTION: Faithfulness to God brings happiness, even amid turmoil. This truth applies not only to war but also to personal challenges such as financial setbacks, loss of employment, the death of a loved one, troubled relationships with family members, and natural disasters. When has the Lord blessed you or someone you know with prosperity, peace, and happiness during challenging times?*

At this time with Captain Moroni, the Nephites were happier than any other time in Nephite history.

> *REFLECTION: Why do you think this was the happiest the Nephites had ever been even with the threat of continued warfare looming over them? How can you make your life happier by following their example?*

Alma 50:24 (Years 5-6)

These were also years of peace among the Nephites.

CHAPTER 5
Year 7 of The War Chapters

Alma 50:25-40

There would have been peace among the Nephites in that year, had it not been for a contention between two lands that bordered each other by the seashore. The people in the lands of Morianton and Lehi were fighting over a piece of land that the land of Morianton claimed as its own, but it really belonged to the land of Lehi.

Morianton, the leader of the land of Morianton, wanted to kill the people of Lehi over this contention. The people of the land of Lehi ran to Moroni's camp to ask him for help since they were not in the wrong. Morianton was afraid of Moroni, so he planned to run north with his army and take possession of the Nephite city of Bountiful. Morianton would have gotten away with this plan, but he got terribly angry and beat up one of his maid-servants, who went and told Moroni everything.

> REFLECTION: *How could Morianton have handled this land dispute and his treatment of his maid-servant better? What qualities would he have needed to handle it peaceably?*

Moroni was very worried that the people of Bountiful would listen to Morianton and unite with his people, giving Morianton more power. He believed it would lead to serious consequences for the people of Nephi, possibly causing them to lose their freedom.

> **REFLECTION: Why do you think Moroni felt that way? To understand, consider Morianton's attitude and way of handling conflict. What would happen if more and more people acted like him?**

Moroni sent chief captain Teancum to stop Morianton's flight into the land northward. Teancum's army was able to head them off at the borders of the land Desolation. Due to Morianton's wickedness and flattery, his people were very stubborn and wicked. Rather than return home, they battled Teancum's army, which led to Morianton's death and the defeat of his army. Teancum took those who weren't slain as prisoners and led them back to Moroni's camp. Once they covenanted to keep the peace, they were allowed to return to the land of Morianton. The two lands of Lehi and Morianton reconciled and were once again at peace.

In the same year that peace was restored, Nephihah, the second chief judge, died. He was a righteous man, as was his son, Pahoran, who took his place. Pahoran vowed to judge righteously, keep the peace and freedom of the people, allow them to worship God as they please, and bring the wicked to justice (Alma 50:39).

During World War I, President Joseph F. Smith declared, *"There is only one thing that can bring peace into the world. It is the adoption of the gospel of Jesus Christ, rightly understood, obeyed and practiced by rulers and people alike." (Improvement Era, Sept. 1914, pp. 1074–75.)*

CHAPTER 6
Year 8 of The War Chapters

Alma 51

In the beginning of that year, people who called themselves king-men, wanted to change the law and overthrow the free government and establish a king over the land. Pahoran, the chief judge, would not allow the law to be altered. The king-men were incredibly angry and wanted him overthrown.

Those who wanted Pahoran to stay chief judge to maintain the rights and privileges of religion by a free government were called freemen.

REFLECTION: Read Doctrine and Covenants 134 to understand the role of government in preserving freedom. Write your thoughts.

The contention was settled by the voice of the people, who decided that Pahoran would stay in the judgment-seat. The freemen were overjoyed, and the king-men became silent at that time, supporting the people's decision.

At the same time the king-men issues were happening, Amalickiah was once again preparing the Lamanites to go to war with the Nephites because of his oath to drink Moroni's blood. Even though he had lost thousands of men through bloodshed, he still was able to gather a great army by stirring Lamanites' hearts to anger against the Nephites and was not afraid to attack Zarahemla.

When the king-men found out the Lamanites were coming, with Amalickiah leading them, they were glad and refused to fight. They were still mad at Pahoran and the freemen. Moroni was angry because of their stubbornness, so he sent a petition to the governor asking to be given power to compel the king-men to fight or die. He wanted to stop the contentions and dissensions so the Nephites wouldn't be destroyed.

> *REFLECTION: Why would contention be a cause of destruction among a group of people? Can you think of any other examples in history? What could you do in your family, among your friends, or in your community to resolve contention?*

Moroni and his army went against the king-men to *pull down their pride and nobility* (Vs. 17) and convince them to support the cause of liberty. Any of the king-men who brought a sword against Moroni's men were killed. Four thousand of these men were killed for refusing to fight for the cause of liberty. The leaders who weren't killed were just put into prison — there was no time for trials at that time.

The rest of the dissenters, rather than die, agreed to the standard of liberty, and hoisted the Title of Liberty upon their towers and in their cities, also taking up arms to defend their country. The king-men were no more. The pride and stubbornness of nobility was gone, and humility and valiance took their place.

> **REFLECTION:** *When have you seen the blessings that come from unity strengthen a family, quorum, or class?*

> **REFLECTION: *Based on what you have read,
> what do pride and stubbornness usually lead to?
> Why are humility and valiance preferred?***

While Moroni was teaching the king-men their lesson, Amalickiah and the Lamanites took over the city of Moroni, which was by the seashore. The Nephites in that city weren't strong enough to defend it, and many were killed. Those who were able to get away fled to the land of Nephihah.

The cities of Nephihah and Lehi prepared to fight the Lamanites, but Amalickiah had a plan to take hold of every city by the seashore. He did just that, taking possession of Nephihah, Lehi, Morianton, Omner, Gid, and Mulek — all lands on the east borders by the seashore. *Alma 51:25-26 seems contradictory because verse 25 says that Amalickiah wouldn't fight the land of Nephihah, but then in the next verse it says that he took that land. Take to heart this message from Moroni on the title page of the Book of Mormon: *And now, if there are faults they are the mistakes of men; wherefore, condemn not the things of God, that ye may be found spotless at the judgment-seat of Christ.*

By Amalickiah's cunning, the Lamanites had taken many cities that had been strong fortifications for the Nephites, and they didn't stop there. Next, they marched to the borders of the land Bountiful, slaying many Nephites along the way.

But things were about to change. Teancum had just slain Morianton and met Amalickiah in his march to Bountiful. Teancum's men were great warriors, so they had a great advantage over the Lamanites. Teancum and his army slew the Lamanites until dark, when everyone was tired and wanted to camp. The Nephites camped on the border of Bountiful, and the Lamanites camped on the beach by the seashore. Little did the Lamanites know, Teancum wasn't resting for the night. No, Teancum and his servant snuck by night into Amalickiah's camp. Teancum secretly and silently killed Amalickiah with a javelin (a lightweight throwing spear), not waking anybody up. He went back to his own camp where his men were sleeping. Teancum woke them and told them what he had done and ordered them to be ready for the Lamanites to pursue. And so, on the last night of the eighth year of the war, Amalickiah was dead.

CHAPTER 7
Year 9 of The War Chapters

Alma 52:1-14

The next morning, the Lamanites saw their king, Amalickiah, dead and Teancum ready to fight. They were afraid of Teancum's army, so they retreated to Mulek, seeking protection in their fortifications. Ammoron, Amalickiah's brother, became the next Lamanite king. He commanded his army to maintain the cities they had already taken by force and bloodshed.

When Teancum saw the number of Lamanites, and their determination to maintain the lands they had taken, he thought it would be unwise to attack them in their forts. Instead, he kept his men around, as if preparing for war. As a form of defense, he and his men cast up walls around the land and prepared places of resort (refuge). Teancum kept doing so until Moroni sent men to strengthen his army.

Moroni ordered Teancum to retain all Lamanite prisoners that fell into his hands as a ransom for all the Nephite prisoners that had been taken. Moroni also commanded him to fortify Bountiful and secure the narrow pass that led northward so there would be no chance for the Lamanites to have power there. Moroni also asked him to faithfully maintain that quarter of the land and seek every opportunity to scourge (drive out) the Lamanites there, so he could take cities back by strategy or some other way. He also ordered him to strengthen and fortify the cities not yet taken by the Lamanites.

REFLECTION: Why do you think all this detail about fortifying and strengthening lands is in the war chapters? How can we prepare to defend ourselves against Satan in our spiritual wars? What may need to be "scourged" or driven from our own lives to help us be more spiritually secure?

Elder Ronald A Rasband said,

"President Russell M. Nelson has taught, 'In coming days, it will not be possible to survive spiritually without the guiding, directing, comforting, and constant influence of the Holy Ghost.'…[We] are at war with Satan for the souls of men. The battle lines were drawn in our pre-earth life…For our safety, we must build a fortress of spirituality and protection for our very souls, a fortress that will not be penetrated by the evil one…When we build a fortress of spiritual strength, we can shun the advances of the adversary, turn our backs on him, and feel the peace of the Spirit." (Ronald A. Rasband, "Build a Fortress of Spirituality and Protection," General Conference, April 2019)

Moroni was not able to come help Teancum's army at that time because he had to fight the Lamanites who had attacked in the borders of the land by the west sea. While all this was happening, Ammoron had left Zarahemla, told the queen what had happened to Amalickiah, and gathered a large number of men to march against the Nephites by the west sea, where Moroni was. His intent was to harass (meaning to exhaust an enemy with repeated attacks) the Nephites there with part of his army, keeping them from assisting anyone else, so that the rest of his army could take possession of as much land as possible by the east sea. It was a dangerous time for the Nephites.

Alma 56:1-20

Now let's see what was happening with Helaman at this time in the war. The people of Ammon had wanted to take up their swords to support the Nephites in the war, but Helaman told them not to break their oath, having faith that the Lord would strengthen them somehow. What immense joy Helaman felt when two thousand of the young sons of the people of Ammon desired to fight in the Nephite army on behalf of their fathers. And so, Helaman marched with his 2000 stripling warriors, who he called his sons, to the land of Judea to support Antipus, the chief captain in Judea, and his army.

REFLECTION: *Think of the implications of Helaman, a Nephite, calling the sons of the people of Ammon, who were once Lamanites, his sons. What does that mean about the definition of family?*

Antipus rejoiced when Helaman and his sons arrived. Antipus had lost much of his army due to the Lamanites slaying them or kidnapping their chief captains. There was great cause to mourn, but Helaman felt that because these men had died in the cause of their country and their God that they were happy.

REFLECTION: *Can you think of others in the scriptures who felt happiness and peace at the thought of losing their lives for their beliefs?*

By the time Helaman arrived in Judea, the Lamanites had already overtaken the Nephite lands of Manti, Zeezrom, Cumeni, and Antiparah. That is why Antipus and the rest of his army were working tirelessly to fortify and maintain Judea. Their bodies and spirits were depressed, *for they had fought valiantly by day and toiled by night to maintain their cities. They had suffered great afflictions of every kind,* and now they were determined to *conquer in that place or die* (Alma 56:16-17).

The army of Antipus was filled with hope and joy as they saw Helaman and his sons. With the added strength in Judea, Ammoron ordered the Lamanites to focus on maintaining the cities they had already taken instead of battling at that time. The Lord favored Helaman's sons and Antipus's army and preserved their lives.

> **REFLECTION:** *The stripling warriors were small in number, but numbers had nothing to do with their success in the war. How can that bring comfort to you, especially if you are one of the only members of the Church in your school or community?*

CHAPTER 8
Year 10 of The War Chapters

Alma 52:15-18

In the beginning of that year, Moroni was marching with his armies towards the land Bountiful to help Teancum and his men retake lost Nephite cities. Moroni had commanded Teancum to lead an attack upon Mulek and retake it from the Lamanites, if possible, but Teancum felt it was impossible to do so while the Lamanites were in their strongholds. Instead of fighting a battle he couldn't win, Teancum returned to Bountiful to wait for Moroni, who finally arrived at the end of the year.

> **REFLECTION:** *Why didn't Teancum fight? Some might say refusing to fight is being a coward, but could there have been another reason? What do you think it was?*

> **REFLECTION:** *In a spiritual sense, we learn from Teancum that if we avoid the adversary's strongholds, we are more able to avoid and resist temptation. What are some places that might be considered the adversary's strongholds, or places where you may be tempted to sin? How can you avoid those places?*

Alma 56:20-57

Helaman's story continues: By the beginning of the same year, the city of Judea was ready to defend itself. Nephite spies watched the Lamanites. They were hoping they would pass by the city of Judea so Antipus and Helaman could help other cities from behind. But the Lamanites did not pass by Judea — they just kept protecting the cities they had already taken.

In the second month of that year, the people of Ammon brought many provisions to Judea. How wonderful that these people were not only blessing their sons spiritually through their covenant-keeping, but also physically by providing supplies for their support. Two thousand men were sent from Zarahemla as well. The Nephites in Judea now had 10,000 men and plenty of provisions for them and their families. The Lamanites were fearful of this added strength, so they started to march forth, as if to put an end to them receiving even more strength and provisions.

Because they saw that the Lamanites were uneasy, Antipus proposed a strategy: he ordered Helaman to march near the Lamanite city of Antiparah, the strongest and most numerous station of the Lamanites, pretending to bring provisions to a neighboring city beyond there. As Helaman and his sons marched near Antiparah, Antipus began marching with a part of his army.

> *REFLECTION: It must have taken a lot of courage to march there. Where did this courage come from? How can you develop such courage?*

Lamanite spies saw Helaman's army, so they started to march against them. Helaman's band then fled north in an effort to lead the most powerful army of the Lamanites away from their stronghold.

Antipus started to pursue them straightway, but when the Lamanites realized they were being followed, rather than turn around, they continued to run after Helaman's army. They wanted to destroy Helaman's little army before Antipus could overtake them. They did not want to be surrounded!

Realizing Helaman's danger, Antipus sped up his army's march to come to their rescue, but everyone had to stop for a while because of the darkness. Before dawn, the Lamanites were chasing Helaman's army again. Helaman knew that his army wasn't strong enough to beat the Lamanites, so to protect his sons, he continued marching into the wilderness. The Nephites and Lamanites marched forward all day until the night.

The next morning, they started all over again, but after a little while, the Lamanites stopped pursuing them. Helaman didn't know what had happened — whether the Lamanites were overtaken by Antipus, or if they were planning to trick and catch Helaman's army. He then asked his sons if they were willing to go against them to battle.

REFLECTION: What a testament of Helaman's leadership that instead of telling his sons what to do, he asked their opinions. Think of a time you were a true leader, and then think of a time you appreciated your opinion being heard by a true leader. Write those experiences.

Helaman said that their response showed more courage than he had ever seen among all the Nephites. These stripling warriors faithfully testified that God was with them and would not let them fall. They would not kill their brethren, the Lamanites, if they would just leave them alone, but they knew they needed to assist Antipus's army so they would not be overpowered. These were the valiant words of young men who had never fought, yet they did not fear death. They cared more about liberty than their own lives. Their mothers had taught them *if they did not doubt, God would deliver them* (Vs 47). They did not doubt their mothers.

REFLECTION: *How can you get to a point where you value the Lord's will and freedom more than your own life?*

REFLECTION: *What are some valuable lessons you have learned from your mother or father (or another parental figure)?*

Elder Neal A. Maxwell explained,

"When a parent's teaching and helping job is done well and when there are receptive children to receive the message, then we encounter those marvelous situations such as the one involving young men in the Book of Mormon who had been taught so well by their mothers [Alma 56:47–48]….The reliance…by these young men on their mothers is touching and profound, but the mothers first had to know 'it' in such a way that the young men, observing them closely and hearing them (as is always the case with children observing parents), did 'not doubt' that their mothers knew that 'it' was true." (That My Family Should Partake [1974], 58–59)

Helaman and his two thousand warriors bravely marched back so they could help Antipus, and they came upon a terrible battle. Antipus's army had overtaken the Lamanites, but they were so tired because of their long, quick march, and desperately needed Helaman's help. By the time they arrived to help, Antipus had tragically already been killed, as well as many of his leaders. The rest of Antipus's army was confused because of their fallen leaders and were about to fall before the Lamanites.

> *REFLECTION: In the spiritual battles of life, what has God given you so that you are not confused about what to do?*

As the Lamanites pursued Antipus's army with great vigor, Helaman and his sons began to fight bravely from the rear. The Lamanite army halted and turned around to face them. When the army of Antipus saw this, they started fighting from the rear. The Lamanites were now surrounded and quickly being slain, so they had no choice but to deliver up their weapons and make themselves prisoners.

Once the Lamanites surrendered, and the battle was over, Helaman was worried to find out if any of his sons had been slain. To his extraordinary joy, not one of these young men had died! They had fought with the miraculous strength of God and mighty power. These innocent young men had somehow frightened and overpowered the vicious Lamanites.

> **REFLECTION: *What did the Lamanites see in these young soldiers that made them shrink? How can you develop these same qualities?***

Because these young warriors caused so many Lamanites to shrink and surrender, there wasn't enough space for all of them. Some of Antipus's army led a portion of the prisoners to Zarahemla, and the rest stayed with Helaman and joined his stripling warriors. Then they marched back to the city of Judea.

CHAPTER 9
Year 11 of The War Chapters

Alma 52:19-40

At the beginning of that year, Moroni held a council of war with Teancum and other chief captains about how to get the city of Mulek back. They sent embassies to Mulek to ask that the Lamanite leader, Jacob, come meet them upon fair ground. He refused, so Moroni planned to draw Jacob and his army out of their strongholds.

> REFLECTION: *In what ways might a family council or a Church council be like a "council of war"? How can such councils strengthen you in your battles against the adversary?*

Moroni had Teancum take some men to the seashore, while he took his army into the wilderness west of Mulek. Jacob's guards discovered Teancum and his small army the next day, so they ran to tell Jacob about it.

The Lamanites weren't afraid of Teancum's small numbers, so they marched against his army. Instead of fighting, Teancum and his men retreated north to the seashore. When the Lamanites saw them flee, they got courage and pursued them with vigor. What they didn't know was that they were being tricked. While Teancum led Jacob's army away from Mulek, Moroni took his army to the city to take possession of it.

The Nephite army killed everyone remaining in Mulek who wouldn't surrender their weapons.

Once Moroni took possession of the city, he kept some of his army in Mulek, and then took the rest to meet the Lamanites who were still in pursuit of Teancum.

Teancum's army kept running until they got to the land Bountiful, which is where Lehi and his army were stationed to protect the city. When the Lamanites saw Lehi, they were confused and tired, worried that if they didn't get back to Mulek quickly, Lehi would overtake them.

The Lamanites started to retreat, with Lehi allowing them to do so, but then they were met by Moroni's army. Jacob's army was surprised and fearful to be surrounded by two Nephite armies (Lehi's and Moroni's), who were *fresh and full of strength* (Vs. 31). The Lamanites, on the other hand, were so tired.

REFLECTION: *How can you become spiritually "fresh and full of strength" so you can withstand the adversary?*

Moroni took advantage of their weariness, and had both armies fall upon them until they willingly gave up their weapons. But, Jacob, a Zoramite, had an unconquerable spirit, so he led his people into battle with exceeding fury against Moroni. He was determined to slay them and cut through to Mulek. But Moroni and his men were more powerful. After much furious fighting and slaying, Moroni was hurt, and Jacob was killed.

> *REFLECTION: In the case of Jacob, having an unconquerable spirit led to his demise. When can having an unconquerable spirit be a good thing?*

The fighting didn't end there. From the rear, Lehi and his men began to fight with much fury — so much fury that the Lamanites in the rear gave up their weapons. The rest of the Lamanites were so confused, they didn't know what to do. Moroni saw their confusion and said that if they would give up their weapons, the Nephites would stop killing them. The Lamanite chief captains who weren't killed threw their weapons at Moroni's feet and commanded their men to do the same.

Many Lamanites refused to give up their weapons, so they were tied up, and their weapons were then forcibly taken from them. They would soon be marched into the city of Bountiful. There were more prisoners than people who were killed on both sides during the battle.

> *REFLECTION: What qualities do you see in this story that led Jacob and his men to be conquered? How could the outcome have been different had they had different qualities?*

Alma 53

After the battle, guards were appointed to watch the new Lamanite prisoners. They required the prisoners to bury the dead of both the Nephites and the Lamanites.

Moroni and Lehi then went to the city of Mulek to take command of the city. Moroni gave the city to Lehi, his beloved friend. Mulek had been one of the strongest holds of the Lamanites in the land of Nephi!

After the Lamanite prisoners finished burying the dead, they were led to the land of Bountiful, where Teancum told them to encircle the city with a strong, tall wall of timbers and earth. Bountiful would be a strong city from then on, and it was where the Lamanite prisoners were held. It was interesting that they would be guarded by a wall which they had built themselves. Moroni had to have the prisoners work because it was easier to keep an eye on them.

REFLECTION: Do you think hard work keeps you out of trouble? How can hard work help you in your life?

Moroni didn't attempt any more battles that year, but focused on preparing for war, building fortifications, and taking care of the Nephite women's and children's needs. During that year, there were Nephite dissensions due to intrigue (plots to hurt each other) among them, making it easy for the Lamanites to take multiple Nephite cities to the south of the west sea. Because of their own iniquity and contention, the Nephites in that area found themselves in dangerous situations.

> **REFLECTION:** *Have contention and hateful behavior ever hurt your life, or the life of someone you love? What are some ways people place themselves in circumstances that are spiritually dangerous?*

Hugh Nibley said,

"So it was a blessing to the Nephites after all to have the Lamanites on their doorstep to 'stir them up to remembrance' — 'Happy is the man whom God correcteth' (Job 5:17). No matter how wicked and ferocious and depraved the Lamanites might be (and they were that!), no matter by how much they outnumbered the Nephites, darkly closing in on all sides, no matter how insidiously they spied and intrigued and infiltrated and hatched their diabolical plots and breathed their bloody threats and pushed their formidable preparations for all-out war, they were not the Nephite problem. They were merely kept there to remind the Nephites of their real problem, which was to walk uprightly before the Lord." (Hugh Nibley, Since Cumorah, 2nd ed. [1988], 339–40)

In contrast to those wicked Nephites, we already talked about how a couple of years before, the righteous people of Ammon wanted to help fight in the war. Helaman had forbidden it because he was worried about them losing their souls. But then two thousand of their good sons had stepped up to fight and chose Helaman as their leader. At the end of the 11th year of the war, those stripling warriors began their march to help the Nephites that had put themselves in danger.

Alma 57:1-5

Helaman continued his epistle to Moroni by explaining that in that same year, Ammoron sent him an epistle, saying if Helaman gave up his prisoners, Ammoron would give the land of Antiparah back. Helaman said his army could take Antiparah by force, and would rather exchange prisoners, for it would be unwise to give more strength to the Lamanites. Ammoron said no, so Helaman started to prepare to fight against the Lamanites at Antiparah. However, the Lamanite armies of Antiparah left to fortify other cities, and so the city fell into Helaman's hands without bloodshed.

CHAPTER 10
Year 12 of The War Chapters

Alma 54

At the beginning of the 12th year of the war, Ammoron wrote to Moroni asking him to exchange prisoners. Moroni was happy because he wanted to be able to support his own people and wanted more strength in his army. Before he showed his interest in the arrangement, though, he first commanded Ammoron, who he called a child of hell, to repent and stop the war, or else the Lord would destroy him and his followers through Moroni's armies. Then Moroni gave his conditions — that he would give Ammoron one prisoner for every man, wife, and child in a Nephite family. If Ammoron refused to comply, Moroni angrily professed he would destroy him.

Ammoron was now also angry and did not fear Moroni's threats. He said if Moroni laid down his weapons and subjected himself to be governed by the Lamanites, then the war would be over. He said he would gladly exchange prisoners so he could better feed his men, and so they could wage an eternal war — either until the Nephites subjected themselves to the Lamanites or until they were extinct. Ammoron claimed to know nothing of God, but if there were a devil, wouldn't Moroni go to hell too for killing his brother, Amalickiah? Ammoron claimed that the war was waged against the Nephites to avenge wrongs done to his people, the Zoramites (as their fathers forced Zoram out of Jerusalem), and to maintain and obtain their rights to the government.

> *REFLECTION: Ponder how Moroni's and Ammoron's motives were different for exchanging prisoners. Read Alma 54:18-20 carefully. How do Ammoron's words reflect Satan's motives in his warfare against God's children?*

Alma 55

When Moroni received the letter, he knew that Ammoron was lying. Even though he claimed so, Ammoron knew that the Lamanites did not have a righteous reason for fighting the Nephites. Moroni refused to exchange prisoners and give the Lamanites more strength.

> *REFLECTION: What do you learn from Moroni's reaction to Ammoron's epistle?*

The prophet Joseph Smith said: *"Satan cannot seduce us by his enticements unless we in our hearts consent and yield"* (Teachings of Presidents of the Church: Joseph Smith [2007], 213).

He also said: *"The devil has no power over us only as we permit him"* (Teachings of Presidents of the Church: Joseph Smith, 214).

Moroni now had to find a way to rescue the Nephite prisoners in Gid without trading for them. He found a descendant of Laman, named Laman, who was one of the servants of the king that Amalickiah had murdered, to trick the Lamanites. Laman and a few men, pretending to be Lamanites, offered wine to the Lamanites in the city of Gid, claiming to be escaped prisoners who had stolen the wine from the Nephites. Through reverse psychology, Laman persuaded the Lamanites to drink the wine — so much that they fell asleep drunk.

REFLECTION: What do you learn not to do from the Lamanites' behavior?

Moroni then armed the Nephite prisoners with weapons, and had his army surround the Lamanites. When the Lamanites awoke, they were afraid knowing they couldn't beat the Nephites, so they surrendered their weapons. Moroni took them as prisoners, took possession of the city of Gid, got his own people back, and added to his army.

The Nephites could have easily slain the Lamanites in their drunkenness, but Moroni was merciful because he did not delight in murder or bloodshed, but in saving his people from destruction.

> *REFLECTION: What do you learn from Moroni about how to treat your enemies? How can you apply Moroni's convictions about bloodshed to the shows and movies you watch, the books you read, and the games you play?*

Since he didn't kill the Lamanite prisoners, Moroni was able to use them to strengthen the fortifications around the city of Gid. Then, he sent the prisoners to Bountiful, and made sure that the city was guarded heavily.

The Lamanites often tried to encircle Bountiful to take their prisoners back, but they were never successful. Sometimes they even tried to poison the Nephites with wine, but the Nephites remembered the Lord and were very careful not to be taken by Lamanite snares. They would always have the Lamanites try the wine first to make sure it was safe.

> **REFLECTION: *How can remembering the Lord help you resist Satan's temptations?***

> *REFLECTION: Alma 55:32 is interesting. It says that "if their wine would poison a Lamanite, it would also poison a Nephite." How can that statement be applied to your life? Think of some scriptures that say something similar.*

Rather than give in to Lamanite temptations, Moroni and his army stayed focused and began preparing to attack the city of Morianton. The

Lamanites had made it very strong and kept bringing in new forces and provisions.

Alma 57:6-36

That is what was going on with Moroni during the 12th year of the war, but what about Helaman and the stripling warriors? Helaman continued his epistle to Moroni by saying that the land of Zarahemla had blessed him and his sons with provisions and an additional six thousand men to add to their army. Sixty more sons of the people of Ammon had also joined them. They were strong and healthy, and desired to battle with the Lamanite army at Cumeni so they could get that land back.

Just a little before the Lamanites were scheduled to receive provisions, Helaman and his army surrounded the city of Cumeni. They camped out for many nights with their swords and kept guards to protect themselves. Each time the Lamanites tried to kill them, which was often, the Lamanites were killed instead. Finally, one night, the provisions came. Instead of the Lamanites meeting them, the Nephites were there to take the supplies and those who brought them.

Although the Lamanites had no support, they didn't want to give up the land of Cumeni. Helaman's army ended up sending the provisions to Judea and their prisoners to Zarahemla. After a few days, the Lamanites finally gave up and surrendered themselves and the city. Helaman's army now had so many prisoners, they couldn't keep control of them. They would rebel and fight, so Helaman and his army had to kill around two thousand of them. They had to do something about that, so some of the

Nephite men, led by Gid, set off to take the prisoners to Zarahemla. Oddly, but thankfully, they came back the next day. There was no time for Helaman to ask Gid why they came back because the Lamanites had just attacked them — Ammoron had sent provisions and an army of men (he always made sure his men had provisions) to get Cumeni back again.

The Lamanite army was numerous, but Helaman's band of 2,060 sons fought firmly and killed all who opposed them. Even when the rest of the Nephite army was about to give up, the sons never did — they were firm and undaunted. They performed every command with exactness. They had strong faith, and it was done.

President Gordon B. Hinckley taught,

> *"You reflect this Church in all you think, in all you say, and in all you do. Be loyal to the Church and kingdom of God. …If you put your trust in the Almighty and follow the teachings of this Church and cling to it notwithstanding your wounds, you will be preserved and blessed and magnified and made happy. You're in the midst of Babylon. The adversary comes with great destruction. Stand above it, you of the noble birthright. Stand above it.'" ("Prophet Grateful for Gospel, Testimony," Church News, 21, 1996, 4)*

> REFLECTION: *Helaman said that his warriors "did obey and observe to perform every word of command with exactness" (Alma 57:21). What do you think this means? How was this obedience an expression of their faith? And what blessings have you received in your life from following a certain commandment with exactness?*

Elder Russell M. Nelson counseled,

"[You] will encounter people who pick which commandments they will keep and ignore others that they choose to break. I call this the cafeteria approach to obedience. This practice of picking and choosing will not work. It will lead to

misery. To prepare to meet God, one keeps all of His commandments. It takes faith to obey them, and keeping His commandments will strengthen that faith." ("Face the Future with Faith," Ensign or Liahona, May 2011, 34)

Helaman's sons and the group of men who were taking the prisoners to Zarahemla were victorious over the Lamanites and drove them back to Manti. The city of Cumeni was retained, but not without much loss. After the Lamanites fled, Helaman ordered that his sons be taken from among the dead and their wounds dressed. Two hundred out of the 2,060 were faint with the loss of blood, but to the great joy of the whole army, not one son died, though all received many wounds. It was a miracle!

A thousand of their Nephite brethren were slain, but none of the sons. Why? Helaman said it was because of their exceeding faith that there was a just God, and that those who didn't doubt would be preserved by His marvelous power. These faithful sons were young with firm minds, always trusting God.

REFLECTION: Who else in the scriptures trusted God during difficult circumstances?

After all the wounded were cared for and all the dead buried, Helaman questioned chief captain Gid as to what had happened on the way to Zarahemla. Gid explained that while he and his men were walking, they came across their own spies who warned them, saying that the armies of the Lamanites were marching to Cumeni to destroy their people.

> **REFLECTION: Applying this warning spiritually, what kinds of warnings have you received from the Holy Ghost?**

The prisoners got courage from this pronouncement and started to rebel against Gid. Because of their rebellion, Gid and his men fought and killed most of them. Those who weren't killed ran away. When Gid and his men couldn't catch them, they marched to Cumeni to assist their brethren in protecting the city.

After telling the story, Gid recognized and praised God for delivering them out of the hands of their enemies. Helaman also praised God and knew that the righteous who were slain had entered the rest of their God.

Alma 58

After retaining Cumeni, the next order of business for Helaman was to march with his band to the city of Manti and overtake it. It wouldn't be easy because they doubted they could draw the Lamanites out of their strongholds. And due to how many Lamanites there were, they also didn't dare attack. They decided to just maintain the lands they had already retaken, and to wait for more strength and provisions from Zarahemla. Helaman wrote to the governor, Pahoran, but nothing came to them, while the Lamanites kept receiving more strength and provisions all the time. Helaman's army waited for many months for help, so many that they were about to perish with hunger.

They finally received some food with an army

of 2000, but that was all, and not nearly enough to defeat an innumerable army. Helaman's army was embarrassed, sad, and afraid, and worried that they would be overthrown and destroyed by the Lamanites. All they could do was pray fervently for strength and deliverance. The Lord assured them that He would deliver them, which provided much peace to their souls, granted them great faith, and helped them hope for their deliverance.

> **REFLECTION:** *Think of some fervent prayers you have said. What are some messages of hope and peace God has given you during challenging times?*

Elder Gene R. Cook wrote,

"It may be that the Nephites hoped for a miracle. Maybe they wanted angels to come to deliver them, as had happened a time or two in the Old Testament. But what did they receive? The Lord gave them assurance, peace, faith, and hope. He didn't directly destroy their enemies, but he did give them the gifts they needed so they could deliver themselves. ...In other words, the Lord put inside these men the will and the power to do what they desired — to begin with a strong resolve and then to see it through. After their prayer was answered, the Nephites went on to secure their liberty. When the Lord instills hope and faith and peace and assurance in people, they can bring great things to pass. This, then, is often what we should look for when we ask for help — not a miracle to solve our problem for us, but a miracle inside, to help us come to the solution ourselves, with the Lord's help and the Lord's power." (Receiving Answers to Our Prayers [1996], 156–57)

Elder Dennis E. Simmons explained,

"If all the world is crumbling around us, the promised Comforter will provide His peace as a result of true discipleship. ... We can have His peace with us irrespective of the troubles of the world. His peace is that peace, that serenity, that comfort spoken to our hearts and minds by the Comforter, the Holy Ghost, as we strive to follow Him and keep His....Just as Helaman discovered in the midst of battle that 'he did speak peace to our souls' (Alma 58:11)... , all sincere seekers can have that same peace spoken to them. That peace comes from the assurances spoken by a still, small

*voice." (in Conference Report, Apr. 1997, 41–42;
or Ensign, May 1997, 31)*

As Helaman's army received this assurance
from the Lord, they grew in courage and were
determined to conquer their enemies, maintain their
lands, possessions, and families, and the cause of
liberty. They marched with all their might to the city
of Manti and pitched their tents on the wilderness
side.

The Lamanites spied on them and assumed it
would be easy to overtake this small army — and
necessary because they didn't want to lose their
support. They began to prepare for battle.

Helaman, knowing the Lamanites were going
to attack them, had Gid and Teomner take sets of
men into the wilderness on the right and on the left
to hide. The rest of the army stayed with Helaman.
The next day, when the Lamanites were about to
attack, Helaman's army ran into the wilderness and
passed by Gid and Teomner; the Lamanites didn't
see them hiding. When Helaman's army passed, Gid
and Teomner quickly cut off the spies so they
couldn't tell the rest of the Lamanites what was
going on. Then, Gid and Teomner's armies ran back
to the city, killed the few guards left behind, and
took the city of Manti back.

When the Lamanites realized that Helaman's
army was marching toward Zarahemla, they were
afraid there was a bigger plan to destroy them, so
they retreated into the wilderness. They camped for
the night, thinking the Nephite army would be tired
and not do anything else until the next day. They
were going to be sorry, because instead of sleeping,
Helaman's men marched to the land of Manti in

another direction and then arrived back in Manti before the Lamanites. As the Lamanites arrived, and they saw that the Nephites were ready to battle them, they were afraid and ran back into the wilderness. No Nephite blood was shed in taking back the city of Manti.

Not only did the Lamanites in Manti flee into the wilderness, but many other Lamanite armies also emptied out of that quarter of the land, leaving the lands to the Nephites. Unfortunately, they had taken many Nephite women and children with them. The women and children who were not taken by the Lamanites began to return to their homes, but there was so much land to protect — too much for Helaman's small armies.

But Helaman and his brethren trusted in their God who had given them so much victory. Helaman said to Moroni that he didn't know why the government wasn't helping them more, but since he also didn't know how Moroni and his armies were doing, he didn't want to complain. Helaman was worried that there might be a faction in the government, but he still trusted that God would deliver them out of the hands of their enemies, regardless of how strong their enemies were and how weak they were.

REFLECTION: What do you learn from Helaman in this situation? He and his armies were suffering, so didn't he have a right to be angry and complain? What did he do instead?

Helaman was staying in the land of Manti with his sons, none of which had been slain. Regardless of their many wounds, his sons stood fast in liberty and remembered God from day to day. They kept his statutes, judgments, and commandments continually. They had strong faith in prophecies of what was to come. Helaman ended his epistle to Moroni, hoping that God would be with him and his armies so they could have success.

CHAPTER 11
Year 13 of The War Chapters

Alma 59

Captain Moroni received Helaman's epistle at the beginning of the 13th year of the war (see Alma 56:1). After rejoicing over his success, he wrote to Pahoran, the chief judge, and requested that men should be gathered to strengthen Helaman's army. He wanted to make sure Helaman could maintain the parts of the land he had regained.

Moroni then began planning how to obtain the rest of the Nephite possessions and cities that the Lamanites had taken from them.

While Moroni was preparing for battle, the Lamanites attacked the land of Nephihah. Their army was so strong and numerous that they began to easily slaughter the people there. The people of Nephihah fled and joined the army of Moroni. Their land was taken over by the Lamanites.

Because he had written Pahoran for help, Moroni had expected men to be sent to Nephihah to help maintain it. After all, it was easier to prevent a city from falling into Lamanite hands than to retake it from them later. Because of the fall of Nephihah, Moroni worked hard to maintain the rest of the lands already recovered from the Lamanites.

REFLECTION: Why is staying faithful in the Church easier than returning to the Church after a period of being less active? Why is it easier to maintain a testimony than it is to regain a testimony after falling away?

Moroni and the other chief captains were full of sorrow, worrying that the Nephites must be making wicked choices since the Lamanites so easily defeated them in Nephihah. They were also worried about the Nephites completely falling into the Lamanites' hands. Along with his sorrow, Moroni was also angry with Pahoran and the government for not caring about the Nephites' freedom.

Alma 60

Moroni wrote to Pahoran again, this time to condemn him and other wartime leaders in Zarahemla. He reminded the men of their duties to provide soldiers, weapons, food, water, and other support to the troops. They had been grossly neglectful: had they sent support like they were supposed to, so much slaughter could have been avoided. He questioned Pahoran as to why the government had been so thoughtless. The letter was filled with chastisement.

Moroni even went so far as to say that if Pahoran didn't repent and strengthen the Nephite armies, he would personally kill him. He would willingly do it so his people wouldn't have to continue to perish with hunger and by the sword. Moroni ended his letter by saying that he didn't seek power, but rather to pull it down. He didn't seek for the honor of the world, but for the glory of his God, and the freedom and welfare of his country.

Captain Moroni was quite upset at Pahoran and said many bold and aggressive things, but he still made very profound points. Do you see them? Look at these verses in Alma 60:

- Vs. 11: If you are lazy and do nothing, God will not help you.
- Vs. 12-13: Sometimes God lets good people die so the wicked can be punished while the righteous *enter into the rest of the Lord their God.*
  - Soon after the beginning of World War II, the First Presidency of the Church stated: *"In this terrible war now waging, thousands of our righteous young men in all parts of the world and in many countries are subject to a call into the military service of their own countries. Some of these, so serving, have already been called back to their heavenly home; others will almost surely be called to follow. But 'behold,' as Moroni said, the righteous of them who serve and are slain 'do enter into the rest of the Lord their God' [Alma 60:13], and of them the Lord has said 'those that die in me shall not taste of death, for it shall be sweet unto them' (D.&C. 42:46). Their salvation and exaltation in the world to come will be secure."* (Heber J. Grant, J. Reuben Clark Jr., and David O. McKay, in Conference Report, Apr. 1942, 95–96)
- Vs. 16: Unity is vital to defeating your enemies because you will fight with the strength of the Lord.
  - Heber C Kimball taught, *"Power dwells in unity, not in discord; in humility, not pride; in sacrifice, not selfishness; obedience, not rebellion"* (Orson F. Whitney, *Life of Heber C. Kimball* [1945], 64).

- Vs. 20-21: Remember all that the Lord has done for you and use the means He has provided so you can be set free.
- Vs. 23: The inward vessel must be cleansed before the outer vessel. Moroni was talking about the government as the inward vessel but think about this in terms of your heart being pure and how that affects your outward self. *See Matthew 23:25-28 for further study.
- Vs. 28: Fear God, not people with authority and power. Sin leads to suffering and loss.
- Vs. 31: The Lord will not allow the wicked to remain strong and destroy His righteous people.
- Vs. 32: The Lamanite traditions are why they are wicked, which is not as punishable by God as leaving what you know to be true for worldly glory and vanity.
- Vs. 36: Captain Moroni shows through talking about his own character that seeking for worldly power, honor and glory is not good, but glorying in God, freedom, and country is.

Alma 61

Governor Pahoran wrote back to Moroni, and his response may surprise you. Instead of arguing with Moroni and chastising him for being wrong about him, he expressed his grief over the Nephites' afflictions. Pahoran then explained that he had to flee to the land of Gideon with as many men as he could because the king-men had revolted against him. They had led away many hearts through flattery, withheld provisions, and daunted the freemen. They even took Pahoran off the judgment-seat.

Trying to still be of some help, Pahoran had sent a proclamation to those in Gideon, asking them to defend their country and freedom. Many did come to help, so the king-men were fearful and didn't fight. But they were still in control of Zarahemla and had appointed a king (Pachus) who had joined with the king of the Lamanites. Pachus's plan was to maintain Zarahemla so the Lamanites could conquer the rest of the land. Once that happened, he planned to be king over all the Nephite lands.

Pahoran then took time to encourage and inspire Moroni, thus showing his loyalty to Nephite freedom and the cause of God. He also had a plan. He asked Moroni to come to him and leave the rest of his men with Lehi and Teancum. He had already sent a few provisions to them. They would use the strength of God according to their faith to go against the dissenters. They would take Zarahemla back to get more food for the armies and end the war.

Pahoran expressed his faith that God would deliver them from the Lamanites and dissenters who refused to repent.

There are so many wonderful messages from Pahoran in this epistle. Look at these verses in Alma 61:

- Vs. 9: Pahoran chose not to be angry, but rather to *rejoice in the greatness* of Moroni's heart. What a great example!
- Vs. 10-14: He talked about how shedding blood was not what they wanted to do, but they had to because of the Lamanites' rebellion and violence. God doesn't want His

people to be in bondage and be under the rule of their enemies — He wants them to trust Him that He will deliver them. Pahoran called to his brother, Moroni, and asked him to resist evil with him. Words would not be enough this time — swords were necessary to retain their freedom and privilege of worshiping God.

- Vs. 15: War should be conducted by leaders with the Spirit of God, which is also the spirit of freedom.
- Vs. 17: God will provide strength to help you in battle as you have faith in Him.
- Vs. 19: Moroni's angry epistle actually helped Pahoran. He then knew what to do. *Think about how anger might be a positive force. We will talk about that more later!
- Vs. 21: Pahoran asked Moroni to strengthen Lehi and Teancum in the Lord so that they would have no fear, but rather know that God would deliver them.

REFLECTION: *You wouldn't think it at first, but Captain Moroni and Pahoran are very alike in their patriotism and loyalty for their lands and people. Look at Alma 60:2, 10, 20, 36 and Alma 61:2, 6, 9. What similarities do you see, and why are they important traits?*

Alma 62: 1-11

After reading Pahoran's epistle, Moroni was filled with joy and courage over Pahoran's faithfulness but was also sad about the rebellions of the king-men. He knew it was time to act, so just as Pahoran asked, Moroni took some men to Gideon. As they marched, Moroni raised the standard of liberty everywhere and gained who he could to his armies.

> **REFLECTION:** *Think about how Moroni raised the standard of liberty everywhere. How can you be like Moroni? What cause are you trying to bring people to? How can you raise this standard?*

Thousands took up swords to defend freedom. When they got to Gideon, Moroni joined forces with Pahoran and became even stronger than Pachus, the king of the dissenters. Moroni and Pahoran went to Zarahemla to battle the king-men. King Pachus was slain, and his men who weren't slain were taken prisoners. Pahoran got his judgment-seat back, and it was time for justice to be served. The men of Pachus and the king-men prisoners were brought to trial. Everyone who would not fight to defend their country, but would still fight against it, were quickly put to death. This was done for the safety of their country. At the end of that year, peace had come back to Zarahemla and the Nephites.

REFLECTION: Thinking of the kind of political leader Pahoran was, what kind of leaders do you believe you need in your country? Write the characteristics that made Pahoran a righteous leader. Make a promise to yourself to search out and follow leaders who also strive to emulate these Christlike traits.

CHAPTER 12
Year 14 of the War Chapters

Alma 62:12-41

In the beginning of the 14th and last year of the war, Moroni sent provisions and armies of six thousand men to Helaman, as well as to Lehi and Teancum. He was such a good and righteous leader, thinking about the well-being and success of his other chief captains and their armies.

> *REFLECTION: How can you spiritually nourish others like Moroni physically nourished his brethren?*

Moroni and Pahoran then marched with some of their men to the land of Nephihah to overthrow the Lamanites there. On the way, they killed many Lamanites, taking their weapons and provisions. The four thousand Lamanites who had not been killed, and were willing to make a covenant of peace, were sent to live with the people of Ammon.

When Moroni and Pahoran got to Nephihah, they pitched their tents. Moroni hoped that the Lamanites would come out to battle, but they wouldn't because there were too many courageous Nephites ready for them. Moroni had to come up with another idea.

At night, Moroni spied to see where the Lamanites camped. They were on the east by the entrance sleeping, so Moroni ordered his army to let down cords and ladders from the top of the wall into the inside of the wall. The Nephite soldiers got on top of the wall and let themselves down into the west side of the city. By the morning, they were all in the city.

When the Lamanites saw Moroni and his army there, they were frightened and started to run away. Moroni's men killed many, took many others prisoner, and the rest got away to the land of Moroni, by the seashore. Pahoran and Moroni got the land of Nephihah back without losing one soul. What a blessing!

Another great blessing was that many of the Lamanite prisoners asked to join the people of Ammon and to become free people. They worked very hard, which relieved the Nephites of the great burden of watching over so many prisoners.

Now that the Lamanite army was shrinking, and Moroni's army was growing (as he got many of his men back), Moroni focused on getting Nephite lands back. He first marched to the land of Nephi. The Lamanites there were afraid and ran away. As Moroni and his army pursued the Lamanites from city to city, they were met by Lehi and Teancum. The Lamanites kept running from all of them until they got to the land of Moroni.

Ammoron, the Lamanite king, was also in the land of Moroni. The Nephite armies surrounded the Lamanites in the south and east, but there was to be no more fighting that night. Everyone was resting because of the exhausting march — everyone except Teancum. He was incredibly angry with Ammoron, saying that Ammoron and Amalickiah had been the cause of this great and lasting war, bloodshed, and famine.

Teancum marched to the camp of the Lamanites, went over the wall, and found the king with the intention of killing him. He pierced Ammoron with a javelin (a light spear thrown by hand) near the heart. But before the king died, he woke up his servants who then chased Teancum and slew him. It was a sad day for the Nephites, for Teancum was a beloved and courageous leader.

REFLECTION: *What did you love about Teancum?*

The next day, Moroni led a march on the Lamanites, slew them with a *great slaughter* (Vs. 38), and drove them out of the land of Moroni. The Lamanites did not dare to return at that time, so the war was finally over!

Throughout these years of war, bloodshed,

famine, and affliction, some Nephites had been quite wicked, but the Lord spared the Nephites because of the righteous. The war had hardened some hearts and softened others.

Elder Dallin H. Oaks explained,

"Surely these great adversities are not without some eternal purpose or effect. They can turn our hearts to God. ... Even as adversities inflict mortal hardships, they can also be the means of leading men and women to eternal blessings.

"Such large-scale adversities as natural disasters and wars seem to be inherent in the mortal experience. We cannot entirely prevent them, but we can determine how we will react to them. For example, the adversities of war and military service, which have been the spiritual destruction of some, have been the spiritual awakening of others. The Book of Mormon describes the contrast:

"'But behold, because of the exceedingly great length of the war between the Nephites and the Lamanites many had become hardened, because of the exceedingly great length of the war; and many were softened because of their afflictions, insomuch that they did humble themselves before God, even in the depth of humility.' (Alma 62:41)

President Boyd K. Packer taught,

"The same testing in troubled times can have quite opposite effects on individuals....Surely you know some whose lives have been filled with adversity who have been mellowed and

strengthened and refined by it, while others have come away from the same test bitter and blistered and unhappy." ("The Mystery of Life," Ensign, Nov. 1983, 18)

REFLECTION: Think about how boiling water softens a potato but hardens an egg. How can you allow your trials to make you more like the potato and not the egg (in softness, not deliciousness)?

CHAPTER 13
Aftermath of the War Chapters

Alma 62:42-52

Once Captain Moroni finished fortifying the Nephite lands that were most exposed to the Lamanites, he returned to the land of Zarahemla and gave command of his armies to his son, Moronihah, so he could retire and live the rest of his life in peace.

Governor Pahoran went back to his judgment-seat and the prophet Helaman began to preach again to bring order back to the church. Helaman and his brethren preached with much power, leading to repentance and baptisms among the Nephites. They established the church again throughout all the land while Pahoran worked on new law regulations and appointing new judges and chief judges.

The people of Nephi once again became prosperous and strong, and multiplied in number. They were humble and remembered the Lord and all He had done for them in delivering them out of the hands of their enemies. As they prayed continually, the Lord blessed them.

*Look back at Alma 45:20-24. The story was about the exact opposite when it came to preaching the gospel. We will talk more about that soon.

Beloved Helaman died four years after the war ended.

REFLECTION: What did you love about Helaman?

Alma 63:1-3

Helaman's brother, Shiblon, then took possession of the records the following year. Captain Moroni also died that year.

> REFLECTION: *What did you love about Captain Moroni?*

You now know what happened during the entire war, and you have reflected on some questions and ideas. But you aren't done yet! It's time to really delve deep into your scriptures so you can apply these chapters even more to your life!

PART II: Lessons from the War

CHAPTER 14
You Can Diminish Satan's Power

The Prophet Mormon said,

> *If all men had been, and were, and ever would be, like unto Moroni, behold, the very powers of hell would have been shaken forever; yea, the devil would never have power over the hearts of the children of men. (Alma 48:17)*

That's a pretty powerful statement! It sounds like we need more people like Moroni! Let's break down what Mormon said about him, and see what it was about Captain Moroni that would take away the devil's power (Alma 48:11-16):

> *And Moroni was a strong and a mighty man; he was a man of a perfect understanding; yea, a man that did not delight in bloodshed; a man whose soul did joy in the liberty and the freedom of his country, and his brethren from bondage and slavery;*
>
> *Yea, a man whose heart did swell with thanksgiving to his God, for the many privileges and blessings which he bestowed upon his people; a man who did labor exceedingly for the welfare and safety of his people.*
>
> *Yea, and he was a man who was firm in the faith of Christ, and he had sworn with an oath to defend his people, his rights, and his country, and his religion, even to the loss of his blood.*
>
> *Now the Nephites were taught to defend themselves against their enemies, even to the shedding of blood if it were necessary; yea, and they were also taught never to give an offense, yea, and never to raise the sword except it were against an enemy, except it were to preserve their lives.*
>
> *And this was their faith, that by so doing God would prosper them in the land, or in other words, if they were faithful in keeping the commandments of God that he would prosper them in the land; yea, warn them to flee, or to prepare for war, according to their danger;*
>
> *And also, that God would make it known unto them whither they should go to defend themselves against their enemies, and by so doing, the Lord would deliver them; and this was the faith of Moroni, and his heart did glory in it; not in the shedding of blood but in doing good, in preserving*

his people, yea, in keeping the commandments of God, yea, and resisting iniquity.

Let's look at each quality one by one. Compare him with yourself and see how you are like Captain Moroni:

- **Strong and Mighty**: He was a powerful man, by his physical appearance and his position, but mostly because he drew people in by appealing to their thoughts and feelings through his profound speeches about liberty.
  - *I have commanded my sanctified ones, I have also called my mighty ones for mine anger, even them that rejoice in my highness (Isaiah 13:3).*
- **Perfect Understanding**: Think of perfect as meaning complete or whole. Mormon said he was like Alma and the sons of Mosiah (Alma 48:18), who had sound understanding because they searched the scriptures diligently.
  - *Now these sons of Mosiah were with Alma at the time the angel first appeared unto him; therefore Alma did rejoice exceedingly to see his brethren; and what added more to his joy, they were still his brethren in the Lord; yea, and they had waxed strong in the knowledge of the truth; for they were men of a sound understanding and they had searched the scriptures diligently, that they might know the word of God. (Alma 17:2)*
- **Did not delight in bloodshed**: Even though he had mighty armies, his intention was never

to kill unless it was necessary. He valued
human life and progression.

- *If it be possible, as much as lieth in you,
  live peaceably with all men. Dearly
  beloved, avenge not yourselves,
  but rather give place unto wrath: for it is
  written, Vengeance is mine; I will repay,
  saith the Lord. Therefore if
  thine enemy hunger, feed him; if he thirst,
  give him drink: for in so doing thou shalt
  heap coals of fire on his head. Be not
  overcome of evil, but overcome evil with
  good. (Romans 12:18-21)*

- **Soul did joy in the liberty and the freedom
  of his country:** He was patriotic and wished
  for freedom for all his people and land.

  - *But whoso looketh into the
    perfect law of liberty, and
    continueth therein, he being not a forgetful
    hearer, but a doer of the work, this man
    shall be blessed in his deed (James 1:25).*

  - *Stand fast therefore in
    the liberty wherewith Christ hath made
    us free, and be not entangled again with
    the yoke of bondage (Galatians 5:1).*

- **Heart did swell with thanksgiving to his
  God:** He was grateful for all the blessings God
  had given him and continued to give him and
  his people.

  - *In every thing give thanks: for this is the
    will of God in Christ Jesus concerning you
    (1 Thessalonians 5:18).*

  - *And he who receiveth all things
    with thankfulness shall be made glorious;
    and the things of this earth shall be added*

unto him, even an hundred fold, yea, more (Doctrine and Covenants 78:19).

- **Labored exceedingly for the welfare and safety of his people**: He wasn't lazy, but rather worked tirelessly, not only for himself, but for his people.
  - *And behold, I tell you these things that ye may learn wisdom; that ye may learn that when ye are in the service of your fellow beings ye are only in the service of your God (Mosiah 2:17)*.
- **Firm in the faith of Christ:** His faith could not be broken. Why? Because of the way he lived and worshiped God daily.
  - *…they did fast and pray oft, and did wax stronger and stronger in their humility, and firmer and firmer in the faith of Christ, unto the filling their souls with joy and consolation, yea, even to the purifying and the sanctification of their hearts, which sanctification cometh because of their yielding their hearts unto God. (Helaman 3:35)*

REFLECTION: How did Moroni's faith in Christ influence his character? How did his faith influence his efforts to defend his people?

- **Swore with an oath to defend what mattered most, even to the loss of his blood:** He devoted his life to serving God and his people, no matter what might happen to him.
    - *He that findeth his life shall lose it: and he that loseth his life for my sake shall find it (Matthew 10:39).*
    - President Thomas S Monson taught, *"Courage becomes a living and an attractive virtue when it is regarded not only as a willingness to die manfully, but also as a determination to live decently."* *("The Call for Courage," General Conference, April 2004)* *Manful means having or showing boldness, courage, or strength; resolute.
- **Faith that if his people were faithful in keeping the commandments, they would prosper in the land and that God would deliver them from their enemies:** He listened to the words of the prophets of old and knew that prospering came from obedience, not from his hard work alone, and that

deliverance came from God, not from his own strength and numbers.

- o *And behold, all that he requires of you is to keep his commandments; and he has promised you that if ye would keep his commandments ye should prosper in the land; and he never doth vary from that which he hath said; therefore, if ye do keep his commandments he doth bless you and prosper you. (Mosiah 2:22)*
- o *The LORD is my rock, and my fortress, and my deliverer; my God, my strength, in whom I will trust; my buckler, and the horn of my salvation, and my high tower. I will call upon the LORD, who is worthy to be praised: so shall I be saved from mine enemies. (Psalms 18:2-3)*

- **His heart gloried in doing good, preserving his people, keeping the commandments of God, and in resisting iniquity:** Because of his faith in Christ, Moroni found his joy from doing these things!
  - o *The righteous shall be glad in the LORD, and shall trust in him; and all the upright in heart shall glory (Psalms 64:10).*
  - o *…the Spirit of the Lord Omnipotent…has wrought a mighty change in us, or in our hearts, that we have no more disposition to do evil, but to do good continually (Mosiah 5:2).*

Captain Moroni was not a perfect man — he made mistakes just like all of us. What comfort it brings that we don't have to be perfect to have power over Satan. We just need to strive to have a firm faith in Christ, keep the commandments, be thankful, study the scriptures diligently, seek for peace, serve others, value life and freedom, and find joy in doing righteousness.

CHAPTER 15
Always Be Valiant and True

The prophet Mormon described the stripling warriors this way:

> *And they were all young men, and they were exceedingly valiant for courage, and also for strength and activity; but behold, this was not all — they were men who were true at all times in whatsoever thing they were entrusted. Yea, they were men of truth and soberness, for they had been taught to keep the commandments of God and to walk uprightly before him. (Alma 53:20-21)*

What a way to be described! Let's dive into each of these characteristics with quotes from church leaders:

- **Valiant for Courage**: Bishop Gary E. Stevenson explained, "*...this describes the conviction of these young men to courageously do what is right, or as Alma describes, "to stand as witnesses of God at all times … and in all places"* ("*Be Valiant in Courage, Strength, and Activity," Bishop Gary E. Stevenson, Ensign, November 2012*)
- **Valiant for Strength and Activity**: Elder Richard J. Maynes taught, "*Being spiritually prepared means we have developed spiritual stamina or strength — we will be in good shape spiritually. We will be in such good shape spiritually that we will consistently choose the right. We will become immovable in our desire and ability to live the gospel. As an anonymous author once said, "You must become the rock the river cannot wash away. ("The Strength to Endure," Elder Richard J. Maynes, Ensign, November 2013*)
- **True:** Elder Joseph B. Wirthlin defined true as "*… 'steadfast, loyal, … honest, just' — all virtues that we should cultivate in our lives*" ("*True to the Truth," Elder Joseph B. Wirthlin, Ensign, May 1997*). *Steadfast means you are firmly planted, even during storms of life. Loyal means showing constant support. Just means the decisions you make are morally right and fair.
- **Sober**: Elder James J. Hamula explained, "*Being sober means being earnest and serious in assessing your circumstances and careful and circumspect in weighing the consequences of your actions. Soberness therefore yields good judgment, as well as measured conduct.*" ("*Winning the War*

against Evil," Elder James J. Hamula, Ensign, November 2008)

- **Kept the commandments of God:** President Thomas S. Monson taught, *"God's commandments are not given to frustrate us or to become obstacles to our happiness. Just the opposite is true. He who created us and who loves us perfectly knows just how we need to live our lives in order to obtain the greatest happiness possible. He has provided us with guidelines which, if we follow them, will see us safely through this often treacherous mortal journey." ("Keep the Commandments, President Thomas S. Monson, Ensign, November 2015)*

- **Walked uprightly:** Sister Ruth B. Wright said, *"The word upright is defined as honest, honorable, straightforward. Thus, to walk uprightly, [we] need to choose to live in an honest, honorable, straightforward manner. [Those] who understand and live the gospel today can walk with assurance and joy and someday will enter the presence of the Lord, walking uprightly." (Teaching Children to Walk Uprightly Before The Lord," Sister Ruth B. Wright, Ensign, May 1994)*

REFLECTION: Think about how you personally can develop these attributes. Pray to Heavenly Father for help in developing the attributes which you lack. Write your impressions.

If you would like to do further study about how to be like the sons of Helaman, you can read these talks:

- President Ezra Taft Benson speaks about drawing closer to your mother, honoring and obeying your father, and strengthening the home ("To the 'Youth of the Noble Birthright'," General Conference, April 1986).
- Elder Dallin H. Oaks discusses how to remain true until the end (in Conference Report, Oct. 1997, 101–2; or Ensign, Nov. 1997, 73).
- Elder M. Russell Ballard pleads with missionaries to join God's army in battling for the souls of man, and truth and right ("The Greatest Generation of Missionaries," Ensign or Liahona, Nov. 2002, 46–47).
- Elder David A. Bednar speaks about being steadfast and immovable just like the stripling warriors were ("Steadfast and Immovable: Always Abounding in Good Works," New Era Magazine, January 2008).

- President Henry B. Eyring, speaking to priesthood holders, admonishes them to be like the sons of Helaman and strengthen their brethren ("That He May Become Strong Also," General Conference, Oct 2016).
- Sister Joy D. Jones, speaking to parents of children, counsels parents to teach their children at an early age to be valiant disciples of Christ ("A Sin Resistant Generation," General Conference, April 2017).
- The First Presidency in 1942 provides comfort and direction to those who are fighting in World War II (Heber J. Grant, J. Reuben Clark Jr., and David O. McKay, in Conference Report, Apr. 1942, 96).

CHAPTER 16
Be Wary of Flattery

If only all the Nephites were like Captain Moroni and the stripling warriors. Most were, but some were enticed by flattery. In the war chapters, there were three men/groups who used flattering words to accomplish their devices. They were Amalickiah, Morianton, and the king-men.

Amalickiah: *... he was a man of cunning device and a man of many flattering words, that he led away the hearts of many people to do wickedly; yea, and to seek to destroy the church of God, and to destroy the foundation of liberty which God had granted unto them, or which blessing God had sent upon the face of the land for the righteous' sake (Alma 46:10).*

Morianton: *...so stubborn were the people of Morianton, (being inspired by his wickedness and his flattering words) that a battle commenced between them, in the which Teancum did slay Morianton and defeat his army, and took them prisoners, and returned to the camp of Moroni (Alma 50:35).*

King-men: *...for they have used great flattery, and they have led away the hearts of many people, which will be the cause of sore affliction among us; they have withheld our provisions, and have daunted our freemen that they have not come unto you (Alma 61:4).*

The Lord and His prophets speak out firmly against flatterers and flattery:

- *A flattering mouth worketh ruin (Proverbs 26:28).*
- *He that rebuketh a man afterwards shall find more favour than he that flattereth with the tongue (Proverbs 28:23).* *Think of Captain Moroni and Amalickiah.
- *The Lord shall cut off all flattering lips, and the tongue that speaketh proud things (Psalms 12:3).*
- *But behold, it is better that thy soul should be lost than that thou shouldst be the means of bringing many souls down to destruction, by thy lying and by thy flattering words; (Alma 30:47 - Alma speaking to Korihor)*

What is flattery anyway? Miriam-Webster defines it as *excessive and insincere praise*. When someone praises you, what do you do? You smile and feel good about yourself. When someone praises you excessively, though, you have a subconscious choice to make. You can either see through the insincerity, realizing that the person wants something from you, or you can allow it to lift your ego, make you selfish, and fill you with a hunger for much more than you have — a hunger which can only be satisfied through wickedness.

In the Book of Mormon, there are many flatterers, from Sherem, to King Noah and his priests, to Alma the Younger (before he repented), to the devil himself, and more! (Read 2 Nephi 28:22, Jacob 7:4, Mosiah 11 :7, Mosiah 26:6, and Mosiah 27:8 to learn more about these flatterers.)

When reading about these people, you learn that flatterers know exactly what to say to get your attention. They lead others towards sin and away from godly habits. Flatterers are idolatrous, meaning they worship things of the world instead of things of God. They have ulterior motives for why they are saying or promising things to you. They want something from you and do not actually care about you, just themselves.

They are also going to be likable people so you will believe them. You must be careful not to let flattering words from charismatic people turn your heart away from the Lord and His commandments, no matter how good their words sound. Look at their fruits. Look at their intentions. Look at in whom they put their trust. Then you will know if you should trust them.

REFLECTION: *Have you ever been influenced by flattering words? Write your experience and what you would do differently next time with this new knowledge.*

CHAPTER 17
Soft Hearts Bless Others

In war times, you don't usually think about love, but it was actually quite prominent amongst the Nephites. It's inspiring to think about. Here are some examples of love being manifested in these chapters:

- Love of others was an abounding purpose of the Title of Liberty with a call to remember God, wives, and children (Alma 46:12).
- The chief captains and leaders had a great love for each other's well-being. They were like brothers, always calling each other beloved. Pahoran even called Captain Moroni beloved after he chewed him out, which speaks highly to his character (Alma 53:2;

Alma 56:2, 45; Alma 58:41; Alma 60:10; Alma 61:14, 21).

- The Nephites had a great love for the people of Ammon, which is why they protected them from their enemies. The people of Ammon loved the Nephites so much that they were willing to break their oaths of never picking up weapons again. And finally, the sons of the people of Ammon loved their parents so much that they took up arms in their place (Alma 53:13-19).
- Helaman called the stripling warriors his little sons. He loved them like his own and led them with the care of a parent (Alma 56:46).
- It was clear that love filled the hearts of the Nephites because they did not delight in the shedding of the blood of the Lamanites or their brethren. They tried their best to be merciful (Alma 44:6; Alma 48:14-16, 23-25; Alma 52:37; Alma 55:19; Alma 58:28; Alma 61:10-11)
- Love was also manifested by sorrow sometimes. For example, Captain Moroni and the other chief captains were sorrowful when they worried about the wickedness of some of their people (Alma 59:11-12).
- When Teancum was killed, Lehi and Moroni sorrowed greatly. He had been a true friend (Alma 62:37).

Hearts are vulnerable, and the fact that the chief captains, the governor, and most of the Nephites were able to keep their hearts soft during the war was a testament to their devotion to the gospel of Christ. Speaking of these soft hearts:

- Moroni was able to inspire the hearts of the Nephites to remember their lands, liberty, and freedom when they were fearful of Zerahemnah's army (Alma 43:48).
- Helaman promised his father Alma that he would keep *[his] commandments with all [his] heart* (Alma 45:7).
- Moroni's heart gloried in *doing good, in preserving his people, yea, in keeping the commandments of God, yea, and resisting iniquity.* And Mormon declared that if everyone were like Moroni that *the devil would never have power over the hearts of the children of men* (Alma 48:16-17).
- Pahoran *rejoiced in the greatness of [Moroni's] heart,* even though Moroni had just censured him for presumed neglect (Alma 61:9).
- Moroni's heart *[took] courage, and was filled with exceedingly great joy because of the faithfulness of Pahoran* after he found out Pahoran was true to freedom and his country (Alma 62:1).

REFLECTION: What thoughts do you have about these examples of righteous, soft hearts? How can you keep a soft heart even during scary or challenging times in your life?

If only soft hearts such as these were the only types of hearts prevalent in the war chapters. Sadly, there were plenty of hardened hearts:

- When Helaman and his brethren were preaching repentance, many would not listen, but instead *grew proud, being lifted up in their hearts, because of their exceedingly great riches* (Alma 45:23-24).
- Amalickiah *led away the hearts of many [Nephite] people to do wickedly* through his cunning and flattery (Alma 46:10).
- *Amalickiah, by his fraud, gained the hearts of the [Lamanite] people* as he became their king (Alma 47:30).
- After he got control of the kingdom, Amalickiah *began to inspire the hearts of the Lamanites against the people of Nephi.* Through his efforts, he *hardened the hearts of the Lamanites and blinded their minds and stirred them up to anger* so they would go to battle against the Nephites. (Alma 48:1-3).

- After promising to drink Moroni's blood, Amalickiah *stirred up the hearts of the people of the Lamanites against the people of the Nephites* (Alma 51:9).
- When the king-men found out that the Lamanites were coming to battle the Nephites, they were *glad in their hearts*. They had no desire to defend their country because they were angry with the chief judge and wanted a king to reign (Alma 51:13).
- Pahoran, speaking of the king-men to Moroni, said that they *joy in [the Nephites'] afflictions* and *they have used great flattery, and they have led away the hearts of many people, which will be the cause of sore affliction among us* (Alma 61:3-4).

REFLECTION: What common factors do you see in the hardening of hearts? What leads to that and how can it be avoided?

163

CHAPTER 18
Stand for Liberty and Peace

Speaking of Captain Moroni's Title of Liberty, Elder Ezra Taft Benson counseled,

> *"This is our need today — to plant the standard of liberty among our people throughout the Americas. "While this incident occurred some seventy years B.C., the struggle went on through one thousand years covered by this sacred Book of Mormon record. In fact, the struggle for liberty is a continuing one — it is with us in a very real sense today" (in Conference Report, Oct. 1962, 14–15).*

Moroni's Title of Liberty stated: *In memory of our God, our religion, and freedom, and our peace, our wives, and our children (Alma 46:12).* This is why the Nephites fought that grueling war. Here is what some General Authorities have to say about each of the things Moroni wanted his people to remember:

God

- Elder Brian K Taylor taught, "*This great war over divine identity rages fiercely as Satan's proliferating arsenal aims to destroy our belief in and knowledge of our relationship with God. Thankfully, we have been blessed with clear vision and understanding of our true identity from the beginning: 'And God said, Let us make man in our image, after our likeness,' and His living prophets proclaim, 'Each [human being] is a beloved spirit son or daughter of heavenly parents, and, as such, each has a divine nature and destiny.' Coming to know these truths with certainty helps us overcome trials, troubles, and afflictions of every kind.*" (*"Am I a Child of God?," Ensign, May 2018*)

- Elder Rex C. Reeve counseled: "*If men and nations did reach up to God with all their hearts, war would cease. If love of God were in the heart, a man would have no desire to destroy his brother. There would be no dishonesty if the love of God were in the heart. If God came first in his life, a man would love his neighbor as himself, and instead of taking from him, he would feel to give to him. In the home, if the love of God were in the heart of the father and the mother, the husband and the wife, and God came first in their lives, there would be an end to selfishness; there would be no discord. Instead, there would be a feeling of how can I help you or what can I do for you instead of demanding my rights and my desires, which often destroys homes. Home is really only the feeling between husband and wife — how they feel about one another and God. Home isn't the house, for the house can still be there when home is gone. If men and nations did reach up to God with all their hearts, the Sabbath day would be a holy day. The desires of men's hearts would be to love and serve God and honor and worship Him. Children come to know God and feel love for Him and His word and His prophets before they can read words if these sacred feelings exist in the hearts of the father and mother and they find expression in look and word and deed. The finest thing you parents can do for your children is to love one another and put God first in your hearts and lives. It will strengthen your home and safeguard your family."* ("Look to God," *Ensign*, November 1982)

REFLECTION: *How can you lovingly express to others that they are literal children of God?*

Religion

- Elder Robert D. Hales said, *"Some are offended when we bring our religion into the public square, yet the same people who insist that their viewpoints and actions be tolerated in society are often very slow to give that same tolerance to religious believers who also wish their viewpoints and actions to be tolerated. The general lack of respect for religious viewpoints is quickly devolving into social and political intolerance for religious people and institutions."* ("Preserving Agency, Protecting Religious Freedom," Ensign, May 2015)

> **REFLECTION: *How can you ask for respect for your religion and the ability to worship as you choose, while also respecting the religious beliefs of others?***

Freedom

- Elder Ezra Taft Benson said, *"Why have prophets of God been commanded to proclaim liberty and lead the battle to preserve freedom? Because freedom is basic to the great plan of the Lord. The gospel can prosper only in an atmosphere of freedom. This fact is confirmed by history, as well as by sacred scriptures. The right of choice – free agency – runs like a golden thread throughout the gospel plan of the Lord for the blessing of his children... Our stand for freedom is a most basic part of our religion; this stand helped get us to this earth, and our reaction to freedom in this life will have eternal consequences. Man has many duties, but he has no excuse that can compensate for his loss of liberty." ("Our Immediate Responsibility," Conference Report, p. 120, October 1966)*

Did you know that the Church has religious freedom resources? You can read them here:

- https://www.churchofjesuschrist.org/study/manual/religious-freedom/religious-freedom?lang=eng
- https://newsroom.churchofjesuschrist.org/official-statement/religious-freedom

> *REFLECTION: Think of the history of how the gospel came to be restored. Study 1 Nephi 13 to see how the Lord's hand helped shape history to prepare for the restoration. How can you help in the fight for religious freedom, as well as other important freedoms?*

Peace

- Elder Dallin H Oaks instructed, *"Many think of peace as the absence of war. Everyone wants that kind of peace. Songs celebrate it, and bumper stickers proclaim it. Many good people promote peace by opposing war. They advocate laws or treaties to abolish war, to require disarmament, or to reduce armed forces. Those methods may reduce the likelihood or the costs of war. But opposition to war cannot ensure peace, because peace is more than the absence of war. For over fifty years, I have heard the leaders of this Church preach that peace can only come through the gospel of Jesus Christ. I am coming to understand why. The peace the gospel brings is not just the absence of war. It is the opposite of war. Gospel peace is the opposite of any conflict, armed or unarmed. It is the opposite of national or ethnic hostilities, of civil or family... We cannot have peace among nations without achieving general righteousness among the people who comprise them."* ("World Peace." Ensign, May 1990)

- Elder John A. Widtsoe said, *"The only way to build a peaceful community is to build men and women who are lovers and makers of peace. Each individual, by that doctrine of Christ and His Church, holds in his own hands the peace of the world. That makes me responsible for the peace of the world, and makes you individually responsible for the peace of the world. The responsibility cannot be shifted to someone else. It cannot be placed upon the shoulders of Congress or Parliament, or any other organization of men with governing authority." (In Conference Report, Oct. 1943, p. 113)*

These entire talks about being peacemakers would be wonderful to review as well:

- Elder Ulisses Soares speaks about developing Christlike attributes so we can bring peace to the world ("Followers of the Prince of Peace," General Conference, April 2023).
- President Russell M. Nelson urges us to choose peace over contention always ("Peacemakers Needed," General Conference, April 2023).

> **REFLECTION: *How can you be a peacemaker in your home, in your community, and in your country? Think about how your simple actions can bring about great things.***

Wives and Children

- Elder M. Russell Ballard said, *"Let me say again that the family is the main target of evil's attack and must therefore be the main point of our protection and defense. As I said once before, when you stop and think about it from a diabolically tactical point of view, fighting the family makes sense to Satan.... When evil wants to strike out and disrupt the essence of God's work, it attacks the family. It does so by attempting to disregard the law of chastity, ... to desensitize violence, to make crude and blasphemous language the norm, and to make immoral and deviant behavior seem like the rule rather than the exception." ("Let Our Voices Be Heard," Ensign or Liahona, Nov. 2003, 18)*

- Elder W. Douglas Shumway taught that *"...parents and children must work together in unity to fortify family relationships, cultivating them day in and day out... Although the adversary seeks to destroy the key elements necessary for a happy marriage and a righteous family, let me assure you that the gospel of Jesus Christ provides the tools and teachings necessary to combat and conquer the assailant in this war. If we will but honor our marriages by imparting more love and selflessness to our spouses; nurture our children through gentle persuasion and the expert teacher we call example; and fortify the spirituality of our families through consistent family home evening, prayer, and scripture study, I testify to you that the living Savior, Jesus Christ, will guide us and grant us victory in our efforts to achieve an eternal family unit." ("Marriage and Family: Our Sacred Responsibility," Ensign, May 2004)*

> **REFLECTION: Think about the type of spouse and parent you wish to be and how you can make sure your family members have the best life they can. How can you strengthen your family relationships?**

CHAPTER 19
Take Oaths and Covenants Seriously

You may have noticed that in the war chapters, oaths and covenants were made and/or maintained by many people, including the heroes *and* the villains. The motivations and conditions for these oaths and covenants varied greatly. Let's review them! The Church's website explains that "an oath is a sworn affirmation to be true and faithful to one's promises. A covenant is a solemn promise between two parties" (*"Oath and Covenant of the Priesthood," https://www.churchofjesuschrist.org/study/scriptures/gs/oath-and-covenant-of-the-priesthood?lang=eng*).

Oaths/Covenants Made by the Heroes

The People of Ammon: They had made an oath to never again take up their weapons of war years before, but because they wanted to help the Nephites in their dangerous afflictions, they were willing to break that oath. Helaman was worried that they would lose their souls if they did, so all those who had made that covenant were compelled to keep watching their brethren suffer (Alma 53:10-15).

The Stripling Warriors: These 2000 faithful sons of the people of Ammon covenanted in their fathers' place to always fight for the liberty of the Nephites and protect their lands, no matter the cost (Alma 53:16-18).

Captain Moroni: This faithful chief captain of the Nephite army swore an oath to defend his people, rights, country, and religion, even to the death (Alma 48:13).

Nephite People: When Moroni made the Title of Liberty, he valiantly asked that his fellow Nephites join him and covenant to maintain their rights and religion so the Lord would bless them. Many covenanted not to forsake their God, fully understanding that if they broke that covenant by sinning, that God would let them fall by their enemies (Alma 46:20-22).

Pahoran: He became the chief judge after his father, Nephihah, died. As such, he made an oath to judge righteously, keep the peace and freedom of the people, grant religious liberty to all, support the cause of God, and bring the wicked to justice (Alma 50:39).

Freemen: These men supported Pahoran and covenanted to maintain their rights and freedom of religion by a free government (Alma 51:6).

Oaths/Covenants Made by the Villains

Zerahemnah and his Army: Moroni boldly required that Zerahemnah and his army deliver up their weapons of war and never fight the Nephites again. Zerahemnah refused to take this oath because he knew he would not keep it. The fight continued because Moroni wouldn't go back on his requirements for peace. This led to Zerahemnah's scalp being cut off. One of Moroni's soldiers held up the scalp saying that Zerahemnah's whole army would fall unless they covenanted to make peace. Zerahemnah finally agreed to Moroni's terms when he realized his men would soon all be killed. Zerahemnah and his army gave up their weapons and made a covenant of peace (Alma 44:8, 14, 19-20).

Amalickiah's Followers: The followers of Amalickiah who didn't get away were commanded to covenant to support the cause of freedom and a free government or be put to death. Almost all of them agreed to it, meaning some did not. (Alma 46:35).

Lamanite Chief Captains: The Lamanites were disappointed that they could not overtake the city of Ammonihah, so they made a determined oath to destroy the people in the next city of Noah. They were shocked that the city was well-fortified — even stronger than Ammonihah had been — and it was led by Lehi, who they greatly feared. But, since they had made an oath, they attacked anyway, to their utter defeat (Alma 49:12-17).

Amalickiah: He was so angry at the great defeat and bloodshed of his men in the city of Noah that he cursed God and Moroni, swearing with an oath to drink Moroni's blood (Alma 49:27).

People of Morianton: After the needless battle that took place between Morianton's army and Teancum's, the people of Morianton were allowed to return home if they covenanted to keep the peace between their land and the land of Lehi (Alma 50:36).

Lamanite Prisoners: At the end of the war, Moroni and Pahoran marched with many men to overthrow the Lamanites in the city Nephihah. They killed many, but those who they took prisoner were required to make a covenant of peace among the Nephites. When they did this, they were allowed to live with the people of Ammon (Alma 62:14-17).

Look at the differences between the oaths and covenants made by the heroes versus villains. While the heroes made their covenants for righteous purposes by their own free will and desire, the villains made either rash and angry oaths, or made covenants out of fear of destruction.

However, what is similar is that oaths and covenants were taken seriously by both sides. There were no instances where prisoners made covenants of peace and then broke them. There were quite a few instances in the war chapters where Lamanite prisoners rebelled, but they had not made covenants of peace. Look at the example of Zerahemnah. Although a wicked man, he was honest in that he would not make an oath of peace that he had no desire or intention of keeping. He didn't take that oath until his desire to live outweighed his desire to conquer.

Let's also look at the people of Ammon. They were the only people in the war chapters who considered breaking an oath. But, since their desires were righteous and selfless, the Lord blessed them through the faith and valiance of their sons. And then he protected those sons through the entire war.

By looking at all these examples of oaths and covenants, we learn that they are not to be taken lightly. We should not swear or covenant to do anything without a sincere intention to follow through. We also learn that the Lord blesses those who make and keep righteous oaths and covenants. Sometimes the righteous die in the service of their God, but they die unto the Lord and enter His rest.

President Boyd K. Packer counseled, *"Keep your covenants and you will be safe. Break them and you will not. … We are not free to break our covenants and escape the consequences"* (in *Conference Report*, Oct. 1990, 107–8; or *Ensign*, Nov. 1990, 84)

> **REFLECTION: *Consider the oaths and covenants you have made with God and others in your life. How are you committed to keeping them? Do you have any improvements to make?***

CHAPTER 20
Righteous Indignation is Worthy Anger

Let's talk about anger. This intense emotion is brought up so many times in the war chapters. Here is how it affected the villains:

Zerahemnah: He stirred up the Lamanites to anger against the Nephites so he could put them into bondage. He was angry because he didn't like the Nephite religion, and then because he didn't like Moroni's terms of making an oath not to fight again. He ended up with his scalp cut off. He was angry again, and his people fell by sword to the point where they were nearly destroyed. He finally made a covenant of peace, but all of that could have been avoided had he calmed down and seen reason (Alma 43-44).

Amalickiah and the dissenters: They were mad because they wanted Amalickiah to be king and didn't like the preaching of Helaman and his brethren. The dissenters who didn't get away with Amalickiah were killed if they didn't support the cause of freedom. Amalickiah stirred up the Lamanites to anger against the Nephites. He used his cunning to kill and get to the top, but his anger did not go away because Moroni was prepared for him. His anger was so great, he cursed God and swore to drink Moroni's blood at one point. Teancum killed Amalickiah (Alma 46:1-10, 29-35; Alma 47; Alma 48:1-6; Alma 49; Alma 51:9-34).

The King of the Lamanites: He was mad that some of the Lamanites didn't want to fight. Amalickiah killed him (Alma 47:3-24).

Morianton: He once got so angry that he beat one of his maid-servants. Because of this, she warned Moroni, and Morianton was unable to flee. Teancum killed him (Alma 50:30-35).

King-men: They were angry because they didn't want Pahoran to be the chief judge any longer. They wanted a king. They were killed if they refused to join the cause of liberty (Alma 51:4-21).

Jacob the Zoramite: He fought with great fury against Moroni, and Moroni's army killed him (Alma 52:33-35).

Ammoron: He was very angry with Moroni because of his epistle about exchanging prisoners. He threatened to avenge his brother, Amalickiah's death, and attack Moroni's armies without fear. Teancum killed him (Alma 54:15-24, 62:36).

It was mostly the villains who got angry, but here are two heroes who also did:

Teancum: He considered Amalickiah and Ammoron the cause of the great and long war, and in his great anger, went in to kill Ammoron in his sleep. He did kill him, but not before waking the servants up, who then killed him as well (Alma 62:35-36).

Captain Moroni: He was angry a lot!

- He was angry with Zerahemnah and his army for being stubborn and not laying down their weapons and taking an oath. He caused his army to slay them but stopped shedding their blood when they became afraid of destruction and pleaded for mercy. (Alma 44:17-20)
- He was angry with Amalickiah for leading away many to do wickedness and seeking to destroy the church of God and religious liberty. This inspired him to tear his coat and write the Title of Liberty, using it to call people to the cause of freedom. (Alma 46:11-36)
- He was angry at the king-men for refusing to fight the Lamanites and defend their country. He had worked so hard to keep them and the rest of his people safe. He got permission from the governor to kill them if they wouldn't join the cause of liberty. He knew that contentions and dissensions among the people led to their destruction. The king-men

were no more due to his efforts, as they were either killed, put in prison, or yielded to the standard of liberty. (Alma 51:13-21)

- He was angry at Ammoron for murdering the Nephites when all they wanted to do was defend themselves. He promised that he would not exchange prisoners unless it was a man for a man, woman, and child, and that he would destroy the Lamanites if Ammoron would not stop trying to destroy his people (Alma 54:4-14).

- He was even angrier at Ammoron after receiving his response to the epistle. He knew that Ammoron knew he had no just reason to fight them, though he claimed he did. He used Laman, a servant of the Lamanite king who was murdered by Amalickiah, to free the Nephite prisoners (Alma 55:1-24).

- Only once was Moroni wrong to be angry. He was angry with the government for seemingly not caring about the freedom of their country. This led him to send an angry epistle to Governor Pahoran. Even though it was full of gospel truth, it was also full of untrue condemnation. Moroni was in the wrong, but Pahoran was actually grateful for the epistle, as it helped him know how to handle the real cause of the indifference: Pachus and the king-men (Alma 59:13, 60).

Almost everyone who was angry in the war chapters was killed or defeated, even Teancum. Why not Captain Moroni? Well, each time Moroni was angry, it was because of his intense love for liberty.

He fought passionately for it, even with the sword. But he never delighted in bloodshed or power. He merely wanted to avoid destruction and to keep the liberty of the people.

Teancum was killed while trying to kill Ammoron. Why wasn't he slain earlier when he killed Amalickiah? It is hard to say, but he wasn't angry that time and it was also a different situation — a fortified city, not a tent; he had to find Ammoron; he had to throw the weapon rather than be able to kill him quietly. After Ammoron's death, the Lamanites had no leader, and were driven out of the land by Moroni's army. Perhaps if Teancum had been less angry, and calmer, he may have succeeded in his task. We do not know, but Mormon took the time to mention his anger twice (Alma 62:35-36). We also know that Lehi and Moroni highly respected Teancum for his valiance and love of liberty (Alma 62:37). It was so sad that Teancum died, but his sacrifice helped end the long war.

There was *one* person in the war chapters who did not allow himself to be angry, even when he would have been justified:

Pahoran: Although Moroni was very unkind to him, he chose not to be angry, but praised him for his great heart (Alma 61).

> *REFLECTION: Read Alma 61. What do you learn from Pahoran's example?*

Elder David A. Bednar taught that,

"… Moroni … wrote to Pahoran 'by the way of condemnation' (Alma 60:2) and harshly accused him of thoughtlessness, slothfulness, and neglect. Pahoran might easily have resented Moroni and his message, but he chose not to take offense. …One of the greatest indicators of our own spiritual maturity is revealed in how we respond to the weaknesses, the inexperience, and the potentially offensive actions of others. A thing, an event, or an expression may be offensive, but you and I can choose not to be offended — and to say with Pahoran, 'it mattereth not.' … If a person says or does something that we consider offensive, our first obligation is to refuse to take offense and then communicate privately, honestly, and directly with that individual. Such an approach invites inspiration from the Holy Ghost and permits

misperceptions to be clarified and true intent to be understood" ("And Nothing Shall Offend Them," Ensign or Liahona, Nov. 2006, 91–92).

What's the bottom line in all this? Be careful of anger. If you are led to anger, be like Captain Moroni and use that anger to further a righteous cause, not to seek revenge and retaliate against others. Or be like Pahoran and choose not to be offended in the first place, but rather see the good in others.

CHAPTER 21
Refuse to Delight in Bloodshed

When you think of delighting in something, bloodshed is probably the furthest thing from your mind. And yet, that phrase is often used in the war chapters. The Nephites, particularly Captain Moroni, set an incredible example of mercy in war, and only shed blood when necessary.

The Lord told the Nephites to defend their families even in bloodshed. Notice how He said to defend rather than to attack. And so, the only reasons the Nephites at the time engaged in war were to defend themselves, their families, their lands, their country, their rights, and their religion — all righteous reasons to shed blood.

> **REFLECTION: How can you defend what's right without being on the attack?**

We learn more about the hearts of the Nephites in these verses:

> *Now, they were sorry to take up arms against the Lamanites, because they did not delight in the shedding of blood; yea, and this was not all — they were sorry to be the means of sending so many of their brethren out of this world into an eternal world, unprepared to meet their God. Nevertheless, they could not suffer to lay down their lives, that their wives and their children should be massacred by the barbarous cruelty of those who were once their brethren, yea, and*

had dissented from their church, and had left them and had gone to destroy them by joining the Lamanites. Yea, they could not bear that their brethren should rejoice over the blood of the Nephites, so long as there were any who should keep the commandments of God, for the promise of the Lord was, if they should keep his commandments they should prosper in the land. (Alma 48:23-25)

What wonderful people these righteous Nephites were! They knew they had no choice but to fight the Lamanites, and their own brethren who had joined them, but they were so sorrowful at the idea of sending them out of the world unprepared to meet God. Even amid bloodshed, they thought of their brethren's eternal salvation. Still, they had an obligation to protect those they loved who were keeping God's commandments and worthy of His prosperity.

REFLECTION: Do you think like the Nephites? How can you apply their concern for their wicked brethren to how you think of and treat others in your life who aren't making the best choices?

Captain Moroni was the epitome of these principals. As the prophet Mormon described,

> *…Moroni was…a man that did not delight in bloodshed; a man whose soul did joy in the liberty and the freedom of his country, and his brethren from bondage and slavery; Yea, and he was a man who was firm in the faith of Christ, and he had sworn with an oath to defend his people, his rights, and his country, and his religion, even to the loss of his blood…His heart did glory…not in the shedding of blood but in doing good, in preserving his people, yea, in keeping the commandments of God, yea, and resisting iniquity. (Alma 48:11, 13, 16)*

And let us not forget the peaceful people of Ammon who had made an oath to never shed blood again! They were so compassionate to the Nephites' sacrifice for them that they almost decided to fight alongside them, breaking their oath. But instead, their faithful sons took up arms on their behalf. These 2000 stripling warriors covenanted to fight for liberty and protect themselves and the Nephites from bondage (Alma 53: 13-18).

What wonderful examples all around! And the actions of all during the war matched these faithful convictions. For example:

- The Nephites had Zerahemnah's men surrounded. They were struck with terror, so Captain Moroni commanded his men to stop shedding their blood (Alma 43:53-54). Then Moroni told Zerahemnah they didn't wish to be men of blood and had no desire to slay them, offering him an option to deliver up his army's weapons and promise never to fight the Nephites again. It took a couple of tries, but ultimately, Moroni was merciful and stopped fighting when they pled for mercy and promised to make a covenant of peace (Alma 44).
- The Lamanites in Jacob's army who were left were confused and unsure what to do after their leader was killed. Moroni gave them an option to deliver up their weapons and go in peace. Anyone who didn't became a prisoner of war (Alma 52:37-39).
- Laman and his band of men got the Lamanites drunk in order to free the Nephite prisoners. Moroni had an option to kill the Lamanites in their sleep, but because he did not delight in murder or bloodshed, but rather in saving his people, he refused to kill them in their drunkenness (Alma 55:19).
- Helaman, Gid, and Teomner devised a plan to get the city of Manti back. Because of their

amazing strategies, they didn't have to battle the Lamanite army and prevented much bloodshed (Alma 58:28).
- Pahoran told Moroni that the Nephites wouldn't shed the blood of the Lamanites if they would leave Nephite lands alone, and they wouldn't shed the blood of their own brethren if they didn't rebel and try to kill them (Alma 61:10-11).

The Nephites, of course, did have to shed much blood to protect themselves and their liberties, but they remained true to the commandment to only fight when necessary to defend their liberties. For example, to get the city of Cumeni back, instead of attacking, Helaman and his sons camped around the city to cut off the Lamanites' delivery of provisions. They slept on their swords, and only shed blood when the Lamanites attempted to slay them (Alma 57:8-10).

> **REFLECTION: Based on the Nephites' conviction to not fight first, how should you conduct yourself when in a situation with a bully or someone else who wishes you harm physically, spiritually, emotionally, etc.?**

The Lamanites and the Nephite dissenters who had joined them had vastly different approaches and convictions when it came to fighting. We know that:

- Zerahemnah attacked the Nephites because he wanted power over them and to put them in bondage. He was also angry at them because of their religion (Alma 44:2).
- Amalickiah cared nothing about his people's blood being spilt, and he also swore after two major defeats to drink Moroni's blood (Alma 49:10, 27).
- When Amalickiah's brother Ammoron became king, he commanded his people to maintain the cities, which he knew had been taken with much bloodshed. The Lamanites loved to overtake Nephite cities, and shedding blood was part of the game (Alma 52:3-4, Alma 56:13-14).
- Ammoron swore to avenge the blood of his brother Amalickiah by attacking Moroni and his army (Alma 54:16).

- The king-men caused a civil war because they desired power and authority. If only they had united with their brethren against their common enemy, the Lamanites, much blood could have been spared (Alma 60:16).

REFLECTION: *What was wrong with the Lamanites and Nephite dissenters' attitudes regarding bloodshed?*

The hateful actions of each of these people and groups were incredibly difficult for leaders like Captain Moroni to bear. He was a passionate man who firmly condemned corruption whenever he saw it. At one point, when writing to Ammoron regarding exchanging prisoners, he threatened him this way:

> *And behold, if ye do not this, I will come against you with my armies; yea, even I will arm my women and my children, and I will come against you, and I will follow you even into your own land, which is the land of our first inheritance; yea, and it shall be blood for blood, yea, life for life; and I will give you battle even until you are destroyed from off the face of the earth. Behold, I am in my anger, and also my people; ye have sought to murder us, and we have only sought to defend ourselves. But behold, if ye seek to destroy us more we will seek to destroy you; yea, and we will seek our land, the land of our first inheritance. (Alma 54:12-13)*

Moroni had had enough, and understandably so. But we know that his anger was always driven by his incredible love for his people, their liberties, and their religion. He kept the commandments and never did delight in bloodshed, even after all the carnage wrought upon his beloved people.

REFLECTION: *How can you stay true to the course even when you see horrible things happening all around you?*

CHAPTER 22
Do Not Let Fear Overcome You

During a war, it is common to feel fear. In the war chapters, it led to actions such as running away, surrendering, or refusing to fight to begin with. Most of the fear in these chapters revolved around the Lamanites, but let's focus on two instances when the Nephites were afraid. The first was during the battle with the men of Zerahemnah:

>*And it came to pass that when the men of Moroni saw the fierceness and the anger of the Lamanites, they were about to shrink and flee from them. And Moroni, perceiving their intent, sent forth and inspired their hearts with these*

thoughts — yea, the thoughts of their lands, their liberty, yea, their freedom from bondage. And it came to pass that they turned upon the Lamanites, and they cried with one voice unto the Lord their God, for their liberty and their freedom from bondage. And they began to stand against the Lamanites with power; and in that selfsame hour that they cried unto the Lord for their freedom, the Lamanites began to flee before them; and they fled even to the waters of Sidon. (Alma 43:48-50)

The second was when Helaman and the stripling warriors were suffering and starving for months without provisions, while the Lamanites, on the other hand, were receiving much support:

And now the cause of these our embarrassments, or the cause why they did not send more strength unto us, we knew not; therefore we were grieved and also filled with fear, lest by any means the judgments of God should come upon our land, to our overthrow and utter destruction. Therefore we did pour out our souls in prayer to God, that he would strengthen us and deliver us out of the hands of our enemies, yea, and also give us strength that we might retain our cities, and our lands, and our possessions, for the support of our people. Yea, and it came to pass that the Lord our God did visit us with assurances that he would deliver us; yea, insomuch that he did speak peace to our souls, and did grant unto us great faith, and did cause us that we should hope for our deliverance in him. And we did take courage with our small force which we had received, and were fixed with a determination to conquer our enemies, and to maintain our lands, and our possessions, and our wives, and our children, and the cause of our liberty. (Alma 58:9-12)

> **REFLECTION: Do you notice similarities between these two stories? What were the common denominators that helped these two groups of righteous men overcome their fears?**

Helaman described his stripling sons this way:

Now they never had fought, yet they did not fear death; and they did think more upon

> *the liberty of their fathers than they did upon their lives; yea, they had been taught by their mothers, that if they did not doubt, God would deliver them. And they rehearsed unto me the words of their mothers, saying: We do not doubt our mothers knew it. (Alma 56:47-48)*

Even people filled with unwavering faith like these young men can be tried and tested to the point of fear. But, with fervent prayer, there is reassurance and hope.

In an epistle to Moroni towards the end of the war, Pahoran provided this loving counsel: *See that ye strengthen Lehi and Teancum in the Lord; tell them to fear not, for God will deliver them, yea, and also all those who stand fast in that liberty wherewith God hath made them free… (Alma 61:21).*

What lovely counsel to all followers of the Lord! Fear need not encompass our lives. Don't Pahoran's words remind you of this amazing verse from Nephi?

> *Wherefore, ye must press forward with a steadfastness in Christ, having a perfect brightness of hope, and a love of God and of all men. Wherefore, if ye shall press forward, feasting upon the word of Christ, and endure to the end, behold, thus saith the Father: Ye shall have eternal life. (2 Nephi 31:20)*

If we learn anything from the war chapters about fear, let it be that with faith, fervent prayer, and a life focused on righteous purposes, our fears can be replaced with hope and reassurance.

CHAPTER 23
The Lord Delivers the Righteous

Sometimes when things go well in our lives, it's tempting to pat ourselves on the back and congratulate ourselves for how well we did. It would have been easy for the Nephites to do this whenever they won a battle against the Lamanites, but they took a different approach. They also had faith in advance that *God* would be the one to deliver them, not themselves. Let's read about some of these instances:

- **After the battle with the Zoramites:** *Behold, now it came to pass that the people of Nephi were exceedingly rejoiced, because the Lord had again delivered them out of the hands of their* *enemies; therefore they gave thanks unto the Lord their God; yea, and they did fast much and pray much, and they did worship God with exceedingly great joy. (Alma 45:1)*

- **After the Lamanites failed to overtake the fortified cities of Ammonihah and Noah:** *…the people of Nephi did thank the Lord their God, because of his matchless power in delivering them from the hands of their enemies (Alma 49:28).*

- **After Helaman and his sons preserved the city of Cumeni:** *And behold, we are again delivered out of the hands of our enemies. And blessed is the name of our God; for behold, it is he that has delivered us; yea, that has done this great thing for us. Now it came to pass that when I, Helaman, had heard these words of Gid, I was filled with exceeding joy because of the goodness of God in preserving us, that we might not all perish…. (Alma 57:35-36)*

- **After Helaman and his sons prayed for strength and deliverance during a time of great hunger and suffering:** *Yea, and it came to pass that the Lord our God did visit us with assurances that he would deliver us; yea, insomuch that he did speak peace to our souls, and did grant unto us great faith, and did cause us that we should hope for our deliverance in him. And we did take courage with our small force which we had received, and were fixed with a determination to conquer our enemies, and to maintain our lands, and our possessions, and our wives, and our children, and the cause of our liberty. (Alma 58:11-12)*

- **When Pahoran gave counsel to Moroni in an epistle:** *But behold he doth not command us that*

> *we shall subject ourselves to our enemies, but that we should put our trust in him, and he will deliver us (Alma 61:13).*

- **After the war was finally over**: *But notwithstanding their riches, or their strength, or their prosperity, they were not lifted up in the pride of their eyes; neither were they slow to remember the Lord their God; but they did humble themselves exceedingly before him. Yea, they did remember how great things the Lord had done for them, that he had delivered them from death, and from bonds, and from prisons, and from all manner of afflictions, and he had delivered them out of the hands of their enemies. (Alma 62:49-50)*

REFLECTION: What patterns do you see in these examples? And what inspiration do you find for your own life?

Elder L. Tom Perry gave this lovely insight about deliverance through our Savior:

> *"His Atonement and Resurrection provide all of us an escape from physical death and, if we repent, an escape from spiritual death, bringing with it the blessings of eternal life. The promises of the Atonement and Resurrection, the promises of deliverance from physical and spiritual death, were declared by God to Moses when He said, 'For behold, this is my work and my glory — to bring to pass the immortality and eternal life of man' (Moses 1:39)." ("The Power of Deliverance," Ensign, May 2012)*

CHAPTER 24
Humility Leads to Repentance

Just after the conflict with Zerahemnah, but before the greatest stretch of the war, Helaman and his brethren preached to the people of Nephi. Then, after the war, they preached again. Let's look at both accounts, and you'll see that even though the approach and intent of their preaching was the same, the people reacted very differently. Here is an account of the people's receptiveness during the war:

Alma 45: 20-24

And now it came to pass in the commencement of the nineteenth year of the reign of the judges over the people of Nephi, that Helaman went forth among the people to declare the word unto them. For behold, because of their wars with the Lamanites and the many little dissensions and disturbances which had been among the people, it became expedient that the word of God should be declared among them, yea, and that a regulation should be made throughout the church. Therefore, Helaman and his brethren went forth to establish the church again in all the land, yea, in every city throughout all the land which was possessed by the people of Nephi. And it came to pass that they did appoint priests and teachers throughout all the land, over all the churches. And now it came to pass that after Helaman and his brethren had appointed priests and teachers over the churches that there arose a dissension among them, and they would not give heed to the words of Helaman and his brethren; But they grew proud, being lifted up in their hearts, because of their exceedingly great riches; therefore they grew rich in their own eyes, and would not give heed to their words, to walk uprightly before God.

REFLECTION: The dissenters' relationship with their wealth greatly affected their receptiveness to the gospel. Though it is not wrong to be wealthy, it is wrong to be prideful because of it. Read 2 Nephi 9:30 and 1 Timothy 6:9-11 to get more insight on riches. Write your impressions.

Now let's look at the people's receptiveness after the war:

Alma 62:44-46

…Helaman did take upon him again to preach unto the people the word of God; for because of so many wars and contentions it had become expedient that a regulation should be made again in the church. Therefore, Helaman and his brethren went forth, and did declare the word of God with much power unto the convincing of many people of their wickedness, which did cause them to repent of their sins and to be baptized unto the Lord their God. And it came to pass that they did establish again the church of God, throughout all the land.

Let's look at some more verses about that time:

> *But behold, because of the exceedingly great length of the war between the Nephites and the Lamanites many had become hardened, because of the exceedingly great length of the war; and many were softened because of their afflictions, insomuch that they did humble themselves before God, even in the depth of humility (Alma 62:41).*

> *But notwithstanding their riches, or their strength, or their prosperity, they were not lifted up in the pride of their eyes; neither were they slow to remember the Lord their God; but they did humble themselves exceedingly before him. Yea, they did remember how great things the Lord had done for them, that he had delivered them from death, and from bonds, and from prisons, and from all manner of afflictions, and he had delivered them out of the hands of their enemies (Alma 62:49-50).*

REFLECTION: What was the difference? Why did the people listen to Helaman's words after the war but not before?

REFLECTION: How can you be more open to the teachings of the prophets today?

CHAPTER 25
Obedience Brings Prosperity

The Nephites believed with all their hearts that if they were *faithful in keeping the commandments of God that he would prosper them in the land* (Alma 48:15). They believed this because it was something their fathers had taught them for generations. While in the wilderness, the Lord promised the prophet Nephi that *Inasmuch as thy seed shall keep my commandments, they shall prosper in the land of promise* (1 Nephi 4:14).

The Lord always kept this promise to the Nephites, so long as they kept their part of the promise. In the war chapters, there were many instances of prosperity:

- **After Amalickiah fled, and Moroni hoisted the Title of Liberty throughout the Nephite lands, there were four years of peace:** *And Helaman and the high priests did also maintain order in the church; yea, even for the space of four years did they have much peace and rejoicing in the church. And it came to pass that there were many who died, firmly believing that their souls were redeemed by the Lord Jesus Christ; thus they went out of the world rejoicing. And there were some who died with fevers, which at some seasons of the year were very frequent in the land — but not so much so with fevers, because of the excellent qualities of the many plants and roots which God had prepared to remove the cause of diseases, to which men were subject by the nature of the climate — But there were many who died with old age; and those who died in the faith of Christ are happy in him, as we must needs suppose. (Alma 46:38-41)*

- **At the same time Amalickiah was cursing God and swearing to drink Moroni's blood, the Nephites were praising God for helping them maintain the cities of Ammonihah and Noah:** *Yea, and there was continual peace among them, and exceedingly great prosperity in the church because of their heed and diligence which they gave unto the word of God, which was declared unto them by Helaman, and Shiblon, and Corianton, and Ammon and his brethren, yea, and by all those who had been ordained by the holy order of God, being baptized unto repentance, and sent forth to preach among the people. (Alma 49:30)*

- **During a time when the Nephites, under Moroni's direction, were busy fortifying**

current cities and building new cities: *And they did prosper exceedingly, and they became exceedingly rich; yea, and they did multiply and wax strong in the land...[B]ehold there never was a happier time among the people of Nephi, since the days of Nephi, than in the days of Moroni....(Alma 50:18, 23)*

- **Helaman, when speaking of the slain in Antipus's army:** *Nevertheless, we may console ourselves in this point, that they have died in the cause of their country and of their God, yea, and they are happy (Alma 56:11).*

- **After the war, when the church had been re-established and there had been regulations made in the government:** *And the people of Nephi began to prosper again in the land, and began to multiply and to wax exceedingly strong again in the land. And they began to grow exceedingly rich. But notwithstanding their riches, or their strength, or their prosperity, they were not lifted up in the pride of their eyes; neither were they slow to remember the Lord their God; but they did humble themselves exceedingly before him. Yea, they did remember how great things the Lord had done for them, that he had delivered them from death, and from bonds, and from prisons, and from all manner of afflictions, and he had delivered them out of the hands of their enemies. And they did pray unto the Lord their God continually, insomuch that the Lord did bless them, according to his word, so that they did wax strong and prosper in the land. (Alma 62:48-51)*

REFLECTION: *Did you notice that many of the times when the Nephites were described as happy were when they had died? Why might that be? Read Alma 28:12 for a hint.*

REFLECTION: *How were the Nephites living to merit such joyful, prosperous conditions, even in uncertain times of war? What inspiration do you receive from their examples to apply to your own life?*

PART III:
Comparing and Contrasting the War Chapters to the Final Nephite Battles

CHAPTER 26
Beginning the Final Nephite Story

The war chapters in the Book of Mormon encompass the longest, most descriptive time of war in the Book of Mormon, and we have discussed and pondered many wonderful messages from these chapters. The war chapters correlate perfectly with a smaller set of war chapters at the end of the Book of Mormon, taking place about 400 years later. This time, instead of having peace and victory, the Nephites were led to their destruction. Let's compare and contrast these sets of chapters, using the topics in Part II that we just discussed.

We won't talk about every detail of every battle with dates and times this time, because the prophet Mormon didn't provide as many details, but there is still plenty to talk about. We will study verses from Mormon 1-8 and Moroni 8-9. These chapters will mean so much more to you than ever before if you apply what you learned from the war chapters to these.

First, let's talk about leadership. We already know all about Captain Moroni and what an incredible man of God he was — so much so that the devil would have no power over the hearts of the children of men if all people were like him.

The leader of the Nephite army, beginning in AD 327, was large in stature, 15-year-old Mormon.. He was also an incredible man of God and the prophet Joseph Smith explained that his name means "more good" (Mormon 2:1, History of the Church, 5:400). Jesus had even visited him, and he truly knew of his goodness (Mormon 1:15). When he was only 10, Ammaron, the keeper of the sacred records, called Mormon a sober child who was quick to observe. Mormon would become the one to abridge and compile the sacred Nephite records, which is why he knew and wrote about Captain Moroni and the rest of the heroes and villains in the war chapters. (Mormon 1:2-4). This alone was a great calling and responsibility for him, but it was also in God's plan that he would lead the Nephites into what would be their ultimate destruction.

> **REFLECTION: *Even though you can't be visited by the Savior right now, how can you taste and know of the goodness of Jesus?***

Now, let's talk about the Nephites and the type of people they were at the time of Mormon. They were quite different from the Nephites at the time of Captain Moroni, who for the most part were righteous and fought for godly causes.

Much to his dismay, Mormon's Nephite army was very unbelieving and wicked — so wicked that the Lord removed His disciples from them. There were no miracles and no gifts from God, and the Spirit did not dwell with them (Mormon 1:13-14). The power of Satan was throughout the land as well in the form of sorcery, witchcraft, and magic (Mormon 1:19).

Alma the Younger had actually prophesied to his son, Helaman, (the Helaman who led the stripling warriors) about the future demise of the Nephites. Here are some of his words:

> Behold, I perceive that this very people, the
> Nephites, according to the spirit of revelation
> which is in me, in four hundred years from the
> time that Jesus Christ shall manifest himself unto
> them, shall dwindle in unbelief. Yea, and then
> shall they see wars and pestilences, yea, famines
> and bloodshed, even until the people of Nephi shall
> become extinct – Yea, and this because they shall
> dwindle in unbelief and fall into the works of
> darkness, and lasciviousness, and all manner of
> iniquities; yea, I say unto you, that because they
> shall sin against so great light and knowledge, yea,
> I say unto you, that from that day, even
> the fourth generation shall not all pass away before
> this great iniquity shall come. (Alma 45:10-12)

Alma was absolutely right, making this one of so many examples of prophecy coming to pass! In the book of 4 Nephi in the Book of Mormon, we learn all about the transition of the people from being righteous, united, loving, and happy after Christ came to a point where there were "–ites" again and slowly everybody became wicked.

There were wicked Lamanites first, while the Nephites remained righteous. But it did not stay that way. Around 230 years after the newly resurrected Christ visited the Nephites, this was what happened:

> And also the people who were called the
> people of Nephi began to be proud in their hearts,
> because of their exceeding riches, and become
> vain like unto their brethren, the Lamanites. And
> from this time the disciples began to sorrow for
> the sins of the world. And it came to pass that
> when three hundred years had passed away, both
> the people of Nephi and the Lamanites had become

exceedingly wicked one like unto another. And it came to pass that the robbers of Gadianton did spread over all the face of the land; and there were none that were righteous save it were the disciples of Jesus. And gold and silver did they lay up in store in abundance, and did traffic in all manner of traffic. (4 Nephi 1:43-46)

Because the Nephites during Mormon's time had abandoned the teachings of Jesus and were instead following Satan in full force, their experiences were completely different from that of the Nephites in the war chapters. There is so much to compare and contrast, and so much to learn. Let's continue, shall we?

CHAPTER 27
Hard Hearts and Loving Sorrow

We saw how most of the Nephites in Captain Moroni's time were filled with love in their hearts, even during intense and bloody war. It truly helped them carry on even with their immense trials.

The Nephites in Mormon's time were not filled with love, other than for their own family members. Otherwise, they were driven by hate and revenge. How did the Nephites and Lamanites of his time get to the point where love was all but gone from their hearts? To know that we need to go back in time to just after Jesus visited them.

For about two hundred years there was *no contention in the land, because of the love of God which did dwell in the hearts of the people* (4 Nephi 1:15). This utopia did not last. As the people who identified themselves once again as Lamanites started to get rich and prosperous, pride started to creep in, and class systems and churches were built to get gain. These collective wicked churches that denied the Christ ...*did multiply exceedingly because of iniquity, and because of the power of Satan who did get hold upon their hearts* (4 Nephi 1:23-28).

These Lamanites continuously hardened their hearts. They sought to kill the disciples instead of acknowledging their miracles (4 Nephi 1:31). They were led by false prophets to build up churches, to sin, and to smite the people of Jesus (4 Nephi 1:34).

After about 30 years of this wickedness, the Nephites too began to be proud in their hearts, because of their exceeding riches, and to become vain like their brethren, the Lamanites (4 Nephi 1:43). So, although the wickedness in the centuries after Christ came began with the Lamanites, the Nephites quickly joined them.

Mormon had no positive things to say about his people's hearts, constantly referring to their hearts as hardened. Because of the Nephites' hard hearts:

- The land was cursed (Mormon 1:17).
- They refused to come unto Jesus with broken hearts and contrite spirits, but cursed God and wished for death (Mormon 2:14).
- They did not recognize the Lord's hand in sparing them (Mormon 3:3).
- Mormon's prayers on their behalf were without faith (Mormon 3:12).

- Their hearts were stirred up unto bloodshed (Mormon 4:5).
- They delighted in bloodshed continually (Mormon 4:11).

REFLECTION: Think back to the rise of Amalickiah in Alma 45:23-24 and Alma 46:1-10. What similarities do you see between him and the Nephites of Mormon's day? Remember his behaviors in the war as well.

> *REFLECTION: How can you prevent your heart from being hardened during times of prosperity? The righteous Nephites in the war chapters were able to remain faithful when prosperous (Alma 50:17-23). Jacob 2:18-21 gives great insights on how they may have done that.*

Mormon's heart was completely different from the Nephites'. In contrast, he was filled with an incredible love for his people, even though their actions were coming from extremely hard hearts.

One manifestation of love comes in the form of sorrow, and Mormon often sorrowed for the wickedness of his people: *And wo is me because of their wickedness; for my heart has been filled with sorrow because of their wickedness, all my days; nevertheless, I know that I shall be lifted up at the last day (Mormon 2:19).*

Mormon was so full of sorrow because of the Nephites' wickedness, but, as he beautifully, yet tragically said:

> *Behold, I had led them, notwithstanding their wickedness I had led them many times to battle, and had loved them, according to the love of God which was in me, with all my heart; and my soul had been poured out in prayer unto my God all the day long for them; nevertheless, it was without faith, because of the hardness of their hearts (Mormon 3:12).*

Mormon knew that no matter how many times he prayed for the Nephites, he couldn't change their fate – that was up to their hearts. And yet, he still did it as an expression of his love for them. He also implored his son, Moroni: *Pray for them, my son, that repentance may come unto them* (Moroni 8:18).

Presiding Bishop Glenn L. Pace said,

> *"This prophet had Christlike love for a fallen people. Can we be content with loving less? We must press forward with the pure love of Christ to spread the good news of the gospel. As we do so and fight the war of good against evil, light against darkness, and truth against falsehood, we must not neglect our responsibility of dressing the wounds of those who have fallen in battle. There is no room in the kingdom for*

fatalism." (in Conference Report, Oct. 1990, 8; or Ensign, Nov. 1990, 8–9)

> **REFLECTION: *Do you ever find yourself loving someone less because you think they are doomed for failure? How can you apply Bishop Pace's words to your life?***

Mormon loved the Nephites until the end – he never gave up on them, and he never stopped caring. He mourned their downfall with all his soul:

> *O ye fair ones, how could ye have departed from the ways of the Lord! O ye fair ones, how could ye have rejected that Jesus, who stood with*

open arms to receive you! Behold, if ye had not done this, ye would not have fallen. But behold, ye are fallen, and I mourn your loss. O ye fair sons and daughters, ye fathers and mothers, ye husbands and wives, ye fair ones, how is it that ye could have fallen! But behold, ye are gone, and my sorrows cannot bring your return (Mormon 6:17-20).

It would have been understandable if Mormon had completely turned his back on his people. He had every right to be disgusted beyond belief at the horrible scene of blood and carnage. Instead, he mourned for their souls.

***REFLECTION:** Have you ever given up on someone? Have you ever turned your back and decided to stop caring about the well-being of someone you once loved? Are you having second thoughts? Write your feelings. Pray for guidance and a heart full of love.*

Other than Christ himself, Mormon was the perfect example of someone who loved with all of his heart and without condition. The Nephites needed him because he was a gentle, humble, thoughtful leader who exercised careful and righteous judgment, cared about their well-being, earnestly prayed for them, and hoped for their repentance. He never stopped caring about his people, even during the times he didn't lead them. These were the most wicked people on earth, yet Mormon never gave up on them until the end. He didn't turn his back. He didn't wish them harm. He didn't curse their existence. May we strive to emulate his Christlike example always.

CHAPTER 28
A Different Title of Liberty

We know that Captain Moroni in a spirit of patriotism tore his coat and wrote this phrase, which became known in all the land as the Title of Liberty: *In memory of our God, our religion, and freedom, and our peace, our wives, and our children (Alma 46:12).*

Mormon knew of this title well, and he said something very similar to invigorate and embolden his men to stand against the Lamanites. This is what he said: *And it came to pass that I did speak unto my people, and did urge them with great energy, that they would stand boldly before the Lamanites and fight for their wives, and their children, and their houses, and their homes (Mormon 2:23.)*

His words didn't sound exactly like the Title of Liberty, but this brings it all into perspective:

And it came to pass that when they had fled we did pursue them with our armies, and did meet them again, and did beat them; nevertheless the strength of the Lord was not with us; yea, we were left to ourselves, that the Spirit of the Lord did not abide in us; therefore we had become weak like unto our brethren (Mormon 2:26).

Mormon's inspirational words could not include what he wanted to include most — what he knew would save his people. He knew they would not listen for a call to remember God, religion, and freedom, but at that time they still loved their families and homes. A leader can only motivate his followers by what is important to them, and Mormon did this just as well as Moroni — he was just dealing with very different hearts and minds.

REFLECTION: *Have you had any experiences where you have had to find common ground to motivate others to a good cause? Did you find that common ground?*

CHAPTER 29
Another Way to Handle Oaths

There were so many oaths in the war chapters, and we learned that the righteous and wicked alike kept their oaths, even if they weren't wise. From Mormon, we learn another way to handle oaths.

Mormon had finally been given permission from the Lord to cry repentance to his people, after over three decades of being commanded not to preach to them. Not long after Mormon did so, the Nephites won a battle against the Lamanites. The people then began boasting in their own strength and swearing by the heavens to destroy their enemies.

After leading the Nephite armies for so long and seeing no change, Mormon was tired. He was done: *And it came to pass that I, Mormon, did utterly refuse from this time forth to be a commander and a leader of this people, because of their wickedness and abomination (Mormon 3:11).*

For about 12 years after his decision, the Lamanites slaughtered the Nephites, and then finally, Mormon decided to change his tune:

> *And it came to pass that I did go forth among the Nephites, and did repent of the oath which I had made that I would no more assist them; and they gave me command again of their armies, for they looked upon me as though I could deliver them from their afflictions (Mormon 5:1).*

Elder Jeffrey R. Holland said of Mormon, *"His faith, his hope, and his charity were irrepressible. He could not abandon his own people. Notwithstanding their wickedness, he agreed once more to lead them"* (*"Mormon: The Man and the Book, Part I," Ensign, 1978*).

Even though oaths are particularly important to keep, Mormon saw that the Nephites needed him, and he would do more good standing with them than away from them. He let his love for his people outweigh his sorrow and frustration for their sins.

REFLECTION: *How might some of the stories in the war chapters have been different if some people repented of their oaths?*

CHAPTER 30
The Worst Kind of Anger Amplified

In the war chapters, we learned that righteous indignation, like that of Captain Moroni, was a powerful force to pursue righteous causes, while anger driven by hatred and revenge only led to destruction.

During the time that Mormon was preaching to the Nephites, he wrote to his son, Moroni and said:

> *...I fear lest the Lamanites shall destroy this people; for they do not repent, and Satan stirreth them up continually to anger one with another. Behold, I am laboring with them continually; and when I speak the word of God*

with sharpness they tremble and anger against me; and when I use no sharpness they harden their hearts against it; wherefore, I fear lest the Spirit of the Lord hath ceased striving with them. For so exceedingly do they anger that it seemeth me that they have no fear of death; and they have lost their love, one towards another; and they thirst after blood and revenge continually. (Moroni 9:3-5)

> **REFLECTION: Think about times when you have gotten extremely angry. How does it affect your ability to love and listen to others? Write down triggers that bring about this anger and pray for help to overcome them.**

Mormon also mentioned the anger of the Nephites when describing the final battles:

> *And it came to pass that in the three hundred and sixty and seventh year, the Nephites being angry because the Lamanites had sacrificed their women and their children, that they did go against the Lamanites with exceedingly great anger, insomuch that they did beat again the Lamanites, and drive them out of their lands. And the Lamanites did not come again against the Nephites until the three hundred and seventy and fifth year. And in this year they did come down against the Nephites with all their powers; and they were not numbered because of the greatness of their number. And from this time forth did the Nephites gain no power over the Lamanites, but began to be swept off by them even as a dew before the sun. (Mormon 4:15-18)*

Did you notice how once the Nephites let *exceedingly great anger* be their driving force that from that time onward the Lamanites had complete power over them, sweeping them off *as a dew before the sun?* This description proves what we already learned from the war chapters: anger coupled with revenge and brutality is not of God and only leads to heartache and physical and/or spiritual destruction.

CHAPTER 31
The Danger in Delighting in Bloodshed

In the war chapters, we were inspired by the Nephites' righteous desire to defend themselves and their freedoms, as well as their sorrow over the shedding of blood. Unfortunately, the Nephites in Mormon's time were like the villains of the war chapters. Mormon said there was *blood and carnage spread throughout all the face of the land, both on the part of the Nephites and also on the part of the Lamanites; and it was one complete revolution throughout all the face of the land (Mormon 2:8).*

Mormon's Nephites:
- Swore to avenge themselves of the blood of their brethren (Mormon 3:9).

- Started the battle in Desolation, and of that decision Moroni declared: *"And it was because the armies of the Nephites went up unto the Lamanites that they began to be smitten; for were it not for that, the Lamanites could have had no power over them. But, behold, the judgments of God will overtake the wicked; and it is by the wicked that the wicked are punished; for it is the wicked that stir up the hearts of the children of men unto bloodshed. (Mormon 4:4-5)*
- Had hard hearts and *delighted in the shedding of blood continually,* leading to constant *blood and carnage* (Mormon 4:11, 5:8).
- *Thirst[ed] after blood and revenge continually (Moroni 9:5).*

We know that the Nephites did not prevail in this war. Mormon described their end this way:

> *And it came to pass that there were ten more who did fall by the sword, with their ten thousand each; yea, even all my people, save it were those twenty and four who were with me, and also a few who had escaped into the south countries, and a few who had deserted over unto the Lamanites, had fallen; and their flesh, and bones, and blood lay upon the face of the earth, being left by the hands of those who slew them to molder upon the land, and to crumble and to return to their mother earth. (Mormon 6:15)*

Even when the Nephites were all destroyed, Moroni explained that *...the Lamanites are at war one with another; and the whole face of this land is one continual round of murder and bloodshed; and no one* *knoweth the end of the war (Mormon 8:8).*

The story of the demise of the Nephites is so depressing. The fact that they got to a point where shedding blood was all they cared about is shocking and sickening. That was one major reason they were destroyed in the end.

REFLECTION: *What can you do to not delight in bloodshed? If not literal bloodshed, what about things that cause spiritual bloodshed/death?*

To the future Lamanites, Mormon wrote:
Know ye that ye must lay down your weapons of war, and delight no more in the shedding of blood, and take them not again, save it be that God shall command you (Mormon 7:4).

CHAPTER 32
Fear Overcame Them

In the war chapters, most of the fear came from the Lamanites. During the very few times when the Nephites or stripling warriors were afraid, they did not let their fear overtake them. Instead, they allowed faith, prayer, and a reminder of their righteous causes to reassure them and give them strength.

Let's talk about the fear of the Nephites in Mormon's time. Here is what happened during one battle:

> *And it came to pass that in the three hundred and twenty and seventh year the Lamanites did come upon us with exceedingly great power,*

> *insomuch that they did frighten my armies;*
> *therefore they would not fight, and they began to*
> *retreat towards the north countries. (Mormon 2:3)*

Because of their retreat, the Nephites were driven out of many lands, regardless of their efforts. Mormon said of this time: *...therefore there was blood and carnage spread throughout all the face of the land, both on the part of the Nephites and also on the part of the Lamanites; and it was one complete revolution throughout all the face of the land (Mormon 2:8).*

The Nephites would have some future successes, but we all know the ending of the war. Mormon set forth the chilling scene just before the final battle at Cumorah where all but about 24 Nephites would be killed, and Mormon would be wounded:

> *And it came to pass that my people, with their*
> *wives and their children, did now behold*
> *the armies of the Lamanites marching towards*
> *them; and with that awful fear of death which fills*
> *the breasts of all the wicked, did they await to*
> *receive them. And it came to pass that they came*
> *to battle against us, and every soul was filled with*
> *terror because of the greatness of their numbers.*
> *(Mormon 6:7-8)*

Contrast this with the sweet, faithful stripling warriors who did not fear death because they knew that if they did not doubt, God would deliver them (Alma 56:47-48). Mormon was also able to keep his fears at bay during the bloodiest, most wicked time in Nephite history: *"I fear not what man can do; for perfect love casteth out all fear. I am filled with charity, which is everlasting love"* (Mormon 8:16-17).

> **REFLECTION: *What were these Nephites missing? Why did their fear of death overcome them? Why was it different for Mormon?***

Consider President Russell M. Nelson's experience on a small plane that caught fire, sending it plummeting towards the ground. Instead of being terrified, he was at peace. He said,

> *"Part of the tranquility I felt as death approached came from my knowledge of the gospel. I was falling to my death. I was surprised that I was not afraid to die. I remained calm. Why? Because I knew that my wife [Dantzel, who died in 2005] and I had married*

in the temple. We had been eternally sealed to each other and our 10 precious children. I realized that our marriage in the temple was more important than any other achievement of my life. Temple clothes were more important than any other uniform I had worn. The temple covenants were more important than any other commitments we had made." (www.ldsliving.com, Aug. 29, 2019)

REFLECTION: What was it that brought President Nelson peace, and what can you do to feel that peace in times of great peril?

CHAPTER 33
Left to Their Own Strength

In the war chapters, the righteous Nephites trusted God with all their hearts, and always humbly acknowledged Him and thanked Him for his mercy and deliverance in all their successes. Do you think the Nephites in Mormon's time did that? Let's read some of their experiences to find out:

- **After a winning battle by the sea in the year 362 AD**: *And now, because of this great thing which my people, the Nephites, had done, they began to boast in their own strength, and began to swear before the heavens that they would avenge themselves of the blood of their brethren who had been slain by their enemies. And they did swear by the heavens, and also by the throne of God, that they would go up to battle* *against their enemies, and would cut them off from the face of the land. (Mormon 3:8-10)*

- **After the Nephites drove the Lamanites out of the city Teancum in the year 364 AD**: *And when the Nephites saw that they had driven the Lamanites they did again boast of their own strength; and they went forth in their own might, and took possession again of the city Desolation (Mormon 4:7-8).*

- **When Mormon decided to lead the Nephites once again**: *…and they gave me command again of their armies, for they looked upon me as though I could deliver them from their afflictions. But behold, I was without hope, for I knew the judgments of the Lord which should come upon them; for they repented not of their iniquities, but did struggle for their lives without calling upon that Being who created them. (Mormon 5:1-2)*

So, the Nephites boasted in their own strength. They swore by the heavens to seek revenge, and they never prayed to *that Being who created them.* They instead looked to Mormon to deliver them — something Mormon knew he could not ultimately do.

REFLECTION: When you boast, what does that show about your heart and mind? How is it hurtful?

Let's read a quote from Elder Neal A.
Maxwell about boasting:

> *"Before enjoying the harvests of righteous efforts, let us therefore first acknowledge God's hand. Otherwise, the rationalizations appear, and they include, 'My power and the might of mine hand hath gotten me this wealth' (Deuteronomy 8:17). Or, we 'vaunt' ourselves, as ancient Israel would have done (except for Gideon's deliberately small army), by boasting that 'mine own hand hath saved me' (Judges 7:2). Touting our own 'hand' makes it doubly hard to confess God's hand in all things (see Alma 14:11; D&C 59:21)." (in Conference Report, Apr. 2002, 43; or Ensign, May 2002, 37)*

As Elder Maxwell testified, God's hand is in every aspect of our lives, and we must confess it. Ammon (the missionary who helped convert the Lamanites who would become the people of Ammon), was a wonderful example of this. See

Alma 26:1-16. Interestingly, his brethren thought he was boasting, but he wasn't!

In the case of these Nephites, even though it was wrong of them to boast, God's hand was no longer there to deliver them. Speaking of one of the Nephite battle victories, Mormon said: … *nevertheless the strength of the Lord was not with us; yea, we were left to ourselves, that the Spirit of the Lord did not abide in us; therefore we had become weak like unto our brethren (Mormon 2:26).*

We know the Nephites at this time were incredibly wicked. Elder Ray H. Wood explained more about the Spirit leaving and being left to oneself:

> *"When a person violates any of God's commandments, if there is no repentance the Lord withdraws His protective and sustaining influence. When we lose power with God, we know of a certainty that the problem lies within us and not within God. 'I, the Lord, am bound when ye do what I say; but when ye do not what I say, ye have no promise' (D&C 82:10). Our misdeeds bring despair. They sadden and extinguish the 'perfect brightness of hope' offered by Christ (2 Nephi 31:20). Without God's help, we are left to ourselves." (in Conference Report, Apr. 1999, 54; or Ensign, May 1999, 40–41)*

REFLECTION: *How does it feel to know that the Lord is with you when you are righteous? Have you ever felt His hand with you? Have you ever felt His hand leave you through bad choices? How will you make sure you live in a way to be worthy of His help?*

CHAPTER 34
Willfully Rebelling Against God

As we learned from the war chapters, Helaman and his brethren preached repentance to the Nephites early in the war and after. Mormon had a different commandment early in the final wars.

He described the situation this way:

> *And I did endeavor to preach unto this people, but my mouth was shut, and I was forbidden that I should preach unto them; for behold they had wilfully rebelled against their God; and the beloved disciples were taken away out of the land, because of their iniquity. But I did remain among them, but I was forbidden to preach unto them, because of the hardness of their*

hearts; and because of the hardness of their hearts the land was cursed for their sake. (Mormon 1:16-17)

> **REFLECTION: Why would preaching to hard-hearted people who had willfully rebelled against God not work?**

Let's talk more about what "[willfully] rebelled against God" means. Elder Dean L. Larsen explained,

"Historically, the drifting away from the course of life marked out by the Lord has occurred as individuals begin to make compromises with the

Lord's standard. This is particularly true when the transgression is willful and no repentance occurs. Remember Mormon's description of those who turned away from the true path in his day. They did not sin in ignorance. They willfully rebelled against God. It did not occur as a universal movement. It began as individual members of the Church knowingly began to make compromises with the Lord's standard. They sought justification for their diversions in the knowledge that others were compromising as well. Those who willfully sin soon seek to establish a standard of their own with which they can feel more comfortable and which justifies their misconduct. They also seek the association of those who are willing to drift with them along this path of self-delusion. As the number of drifting individuals increases, their influence becomes more powerful. It might be described as the 'great and spacious building syndrome.' The drifting is the more dangerous when its adherents continue to overtly identify with and participate with the group that conforms to the Lord's way. Values and standards that were once clear become clouded and uncertain. The norm of behavior begins to reflect this beclouding of true principles. Conduct that would once have caused revulsion and alarm now becomes somewhat commonplace." ("Likening the Scriptures unto Us," in Monte S. Nyman and Charles D. Tate Jr., eds., Alma, the Testimony of the Word [1992], 8)

> **REFLECTION:** *Have you seen any of this drifting happen with your friends and family? Have you ever had this temptation? Write down any experience you have with this as well as goals to make sure you do not get to the point of willfully rebelling against God.*

Over three decades after the Lord gave the commandment not to preach, He, in His infinite mercy, gave the Nephites one more opportunity to repent before their imminent destruction. Mormon told this story:

> *And it came to pass that the Lord did say unto me: Cry unto this people — Repent ye, and*

come unto me, and be ye baptized, and build up again my church, and ye shall be spared. And I did cry unto this people, but it was in vain; and they did not realize that it was the Lord that had spared them, and granted unto them a chance for repentance. And behold they did harden their hearts against the Lord their God. (Mormon 3:2-3)

You may remember this is the time when instead of repenting, the Nephites boasted in their own strength and swore to kill off the Lamanites, which led Mormon to stop leading them. The Lord came to Mormon at this time, proclaiming: *Vengeance is mine, and I will repay; and because this people repented not after I had delivered them, behold, they shall be cut off from the face of the earth. (Mormon 3:15)*

REFLECTION: Why did the Lord finally decide to destroy the Nephites? Think of all the times He had been merciful in humbling them, giving them opportunities to repent, and delivering them. What was different this time?

Mormon was sure now that his people would be destroyed. Speaking to the future Gentiles and descendants of the House of Israel who would one day read the Book of Mormon, he prophesied: *For I know that such will sorrow for the calamity of the house of Israel; yea, they will sorrow for the destruction of this people; they will sorrow that this people had not repented that they might have been clasped in the arms of Jesus (Mormon 5:11).*

What a beautiful image — being "clasped in the arms of Jesus." Elder Neal A. Maxwell eloquently explained,

> *"In the anguishing process of repentance, we may sometimes feel God has deserted us. The reality is that our behavior has isolated us from him. Thus, while we are turning away from evil but have not yet turned fully to God, we are especially vulnerable. Yet we must not give up, but instead, reach out to God's awaiting arm of mercy, which is outstretched "all the day long." (Neal A. Maxwell, "Repentance," Ensign, October 1991)*

> **REFLECTION:** *Repentance is never easy, but as we have now learned, it is essential. Think of anything you need to repent of. Write it down and pray for how to become clean and be "clasped in the arms of Jesus" once again. Read Moroni 8:26 for a hopeful message about repentance.*

CHAPTER 35
Wickedness and Cursed Lands

In the war chapters, we discussed the happiness, peace, and prosperity that came to the Nephites according to their righteousness. Let's revisit some of Mormon's commentary from that time:

> And thus we see how merciful and just are all the dealings of the Lord, to the fulfilling of all his words unto the children of men; yea, we can behold that his words are verified, even at this time, which he spake unto Lehi, saying: Blessed art thou and thy children; and they shall be blessed, inasmuch as they shall keep
> my commandments they shall prosper in the land.

But remember, inasmuch as they will not keep my commandments they shall be cut off from the presence of the Lord. And we see that these promises have been verified to the people of Nephi; for it has been their quarrelings and their contentions, yea, their murderings, and their plunderings, their idolatry, their whoredoms, and their abominations, which were among themselves, which brought upon them their wars and their destructions. And those who were faithful in keeping the commandments of the Lord were delivered at all times, whilst thousands of their wicked brethren have been consigned to bondage, or to perish by the sword, or to dwindle in unbelief, and mingle with the Lamanites. (Alma 50:19-22)

Mormon was very aware of the idea of being *cut off from the presence of the* Lord because of his people's wickedness. It must have been so incredibly sad for Mormon, having read about the history of the Nephites since they came to the Promised Land, knowing of the prosperous and happy times that came from righteousness and love of God, and that it was not to be in his time. He surely mourned the fact that just a few hundred years earlier, after Christ had come, that:

...there was no contention in the land, because of the love of God which did dwell in the hearts of the people. And there were no ᵃenvyings, nor strifes, nor tumults, nor whoredoms, nor lyings, nor murders, nor any manner of lasciviousness; and surely there could not be a happier people among all the people who had been created by the hand of God. There were no

robbers, nor murderers, neither were there Lamanites, nor any manner of -ites; but they were in one, the children of Christ, and heirs to the kingdom of God. (4 Nephi 1:15-17)

We already know how the people became Lamanites and Nephites again, both turning to awful wickedness. Let's see what the Lord allowed to happen because of it. Mormon explained,

…[B]ecause of the hardness of their hearts the land was cursed for their sake. And these Gadianton robbers, who were among the Lamanites, did infest the land, insomuch that the inhabitants thereof began to hide up their treasures in the earth; and they became slippery, because the Lord had cursed the land, that they could not hold them, nor retain them again (Mormon 1:17-18).

REFLECTION: Why do you think the Lord *chose to curse the land in this particular way? What other ways has the Lord cursed the land in the scriptures or in modern times?*

None of this should have surprised Mormon, who knew the words of Alma the Younger, who told his son, Helaman:

> *Thus saith the Lord God — Cursed shall be the land, yea, this land, unto every nation, kindred, tongue, and people, unto destruction, which do wickedly, when they are fully ripe; and as I have said so shall it be; for this is the cursing and the blessing of God upon the land, for the Lord cannot look upon sin with the least degree of allowance. (Alma 45:16)*

The Nephites were so sorrowful that they couldn't hold onto their belongings that Mormon thought they were beginning to repent of their iniquities. He was so happy, until he realized:

> *…their sorrowing was not unto repentance, because of the goodness of God; but it was rather the sorrowing of the damned, because the Lord would not always suffer them to take happiness in sin. And they did not come unto Jesus with broken hearts and contrite spirits, but they did curse God, and wish to die. Nevertheless*

*they would struggle with the sword for their lives.
And it came to pass that my sorrow did return
unto me again, and I saw that the day of grace was
passed with them, both temporally and spiritually;
for I saw thousands of them hewn down in
open rebellion against their God, and heaped up
as dung upon the face of the land... (Mormon 2:10-
15)*

Let's talk about some of the things in these loaded, heartbreaking verses:

- **"Sorrowing unto Repentance"** - President Ezra Taft Benson taught: *"Godly sorrow is a gift of the Spirit. It is a deep realization that our actions have offended our Father and our God. It is the sharp and keen awareness that our behavior caused the Savior, He who knew no sin, even the greatest of all, to endure agony and suffering. Our sins caused Him to bleed at every pore. This very real mental and spiritual anguish is what the scriptures refer to as having 'a broken heart and a contrite spirit' (D&C 20:37). Such a spirit is the absolute prerequisite for true repentance."* (The Teachings of Ezra Taft Benson [1988], 72)
- **"Sorrowing of the Damned"** – Elder Neal A. Maxwell called this "false remorse." He said it *"...is like fondling our failings. In ritual regret, we mourn our mistakes but without mending them"* (in Conference Report, Oct. 1991, 40; or Ensign, Nov. 1991, 31).
- **"Happiness in Sin"** – Doesn't this phrase remind you of a very poignant point Alma the Younger gave to his son Corianton regarding the resurrection? Here it is: *Do not suppose, because it*

has been spoken concerning restoration, that ye shall be restored from sin to happiness. Behold, I say unto you, wickedness never was happiness (Alma 41:10). How right he was!

- **"Day of Grace Was Passed"** - President Spencer W. Kimball explained, *"It is true that the great principle of repentance is always available, but for the wicked and rebellious there are serious reservations to this statement. For instance, sin is intensely habit-forming and sometimes moves men to the tragic point of no return. ... As the transgressor moves deeper and deeper in his sin, and the error is entrenched more deeply and the will to change is weakened, it becomes increasingly near-hopeless, and he skids down and down until either he does not want to climb back or he has lost the power to do so."* (The Miracle of Forgiveness [1969], 117)

REFLECTION: Consider how Mormon was able to avoid becoming just like his people. Read his words to his son, Moroni in Moroni 9:25. Write your impressions of his loving counsel.

Tragically, it never got better with the Nephites. Mormon said of his people: *And there never had been so great wickedness among all the children of Lehi, nor even among all the house of Israel, according to the words of the Lord, as was among this people (Mormon 4:12).*

The blood and carnage continued without ceasing until that fateful day, four hundred years after Christ had visited the Nephite lands, when the Nephites were no more. Moroni, the only one left, told this story:

> *And behold, the Lamanites have hunted my people, the Nephites, down from city to city and from place to place, even until they are no more; and great has been their fall; yea, great and marvelous is the destruction of my people, the Nephites. (Mormon 8:7)*

Perhaps the most telling verse throughout all this time of the final war is this from Moroni: *And behold, it is the hand of the Lord which hath done it (Mormon 8:8).*

REFLECTION: What do you learn from this final verse? Why would that be? Could anything have stopped this destruction?

> *REFLECTION: Take a few minutes and write down the value of comparing and contrasting the war chapters to the final Nephite war. What did you learn? What did you feel? What questions do you still have that you can study and pray about further?*

Your Conclusions

President Gordon B. Hinckley's words help wrap up all we have been discussing:

> *"There is [a] war that has gone on since before the world was created and which is likely to continue for a long time yet to come. …That war … is the war between truth and error, between agency and compulsion, between the followers of Christ and those who have denied Him. His enemies have used every stratagem in that conflict. …It is as it was in the beginning. … The victims who fall are as precious as those who have fallen in the past. It is an ongoing battle. …The war goes on. … It is waged in our own lives, day in and day out, in our homes, in our work, in our school associations; it is waged over questions of love and respect, of loyalty and fidelity, of obedience and integrity. We are all involved in it. … We are winning, and the future never looked brighter."* *("The War We Are Winning," Ensign, Nov. 1986, 42, 44–45)*

> **REFLECTION: What are your conclusions as to why the prophet Mormon felt it so important to include these great war chapters in his abridgement of the Nephite records? What lessons have you learned from studying them?**

Hopefully from studying the war chapters so well, you understand that you are a part of God's army, fighting valiantly against Satan's efforts to thwart God's plan for each of us to gain immortality and eternal life. You can help bring others to God's army so that together, we can all strive for the blessing of eternal life with our Heavenly Parents and with our brother and Savior, Jesus Christ.

APPENDIX

Timeline of the War Chapters

Year 1 of the War Chapters (74BC/18th Year of the Reign of the Judges): The war began because the wicked Zoramites were angry that the people of Ammon had taken in the poor that they had just cast out of their land for believing the words of the prophet Alma. The Zoramites had joined the Lamanites and were led into battle by Zerahemnah. He and his army were defeated by Captain Moroni's and Lehi's armies at the river Sidon.

Year 2 of the War Chapters (73BC/19th Year of the Reign of the Judges): Helaman and his brethren preached repentance among the people. Some Nephites got angry and rebelled. One man, Amalickiah, desired to be king. Moroni made, raised, and hoisted the Title of Liberty throughout all the land and brought peace back to the Nephites. Amalickiah, who had run off to the Lamanites, used cunning and deceit to become the Lamanite king. He prepared for war very differently than Moroni and had quite different reasons for fighting. The Lamanites unsuccessfully tried to take over the cities of Ammonihah and Noah. Amalickiah cursed God and swore to drink Moroni's blood. The Nephites were grateful to God for delivering them, and there was peace and prosperity in the Church.

Year 3 of the War Chapters (72BC/20th Year of the Reign of the Judges): Captain Moroni was hard at work building fortifications and towers around every Nephite city. His armies drove the Lamanites out of the east wilderness back into their own lands, and then the Nephites populated that area. Moroni cut off Lamanite strongholds and made a clear dividing line between the Nephite and Lamanite lands. His armies increased daily. Many new Nephite cities were built.

Year 4 of the War Chapters (71BC/21st Year of the Reign of the Judges): The Nephites prospered with wealth, strength, and children. This was the happiest time in Nephite history.

Years 5-6 of the War Chapters (70-69BC/22nd-23rd Year of the Reign of the Judges): There was much peace among the Nephites.

Year 7 of the War Chapters (68 BC/24th Year of the Reign of the Judges): Contention began between the lands of Morianton and Lehi. Teancum defeated Morianton. Chief Judge Nephihah died and his son, Pahoran, took the judgment-seat.

Year 8 of the War Chapters (67 BC/25th Year of the Reign of the Judges): Contention began between those who wanted a king (king-men) and those who supported Pahoran (freemen). The king-men refused to fight when Amalickiah came to attack. Moroni compelled them to fight or die. The king-men were no more (at least for the time being). Amalickiah took over the city of Moroni and many other cities. On his way to Bountiful, Teancum's army met him. Teancum slew Amalickiah by night.

Year 9 of the War Chapters (66 BC/26th Year of the Reign of the Judges): The Lamanites retreated to

Mulek. Ammoron replaced Amalickiah as Lamanite king. Teancum fortified, secured, and strengthened lands, and retained Lamanite prisoners as ransom. Ammoron prepared to attack Moroni's army by the west sea. Helaman and his sons marched to Judea to support Antipus. Ammoron did not overtake Judea but maintained lands he had already taken.

Year 10 of the War Chapters (65 BC/27th Year of the Reign of the Judges): Teancum waited for Moroni's help to take Mulek back. Antipus and Helaman strategized to defeat the Lamanites before they took over Judea. Antipus died in battle.

Year 11 of the War Chapters (64 BC/28th Year of the Reign of the Judges): Moroni, Teancum, and Lehi took back the city of Mulek from Jacob the Lamanite, who was killed in battle. The Nephites took many prisoners in this battle who buried the dead and helped fortify Bountiful. There were also many Nephite dissensions, so the Lamanites took several Nephite cities. Helaman's army marched to the south border by the west sea to help the Nephites. Helaman got an epistle from Ammoron saying he would give back Antiparah if Helaman gave his prisoners back. Helaman wanted to exchange prisoners instead, but Ammoron said no. Helaman took over Antiparah easily, as the Lamanites had left.

Year 12 of the War Chapters (63 BC/29th Year of the Reign of the Judges): Ammoron and Moroni sent each other angry epistles about exchanging prisoners. Laman and others pretended to be Lamanites to trick the Lamanites into drinking too much. That way they could rescue the Nephite prisoners in Gid and then take the Lamanites prisoner. At this time Helaman's army was strong and took Cumeni by cutting off Lamanite provisions. Prisoners got out of control. Lamanites tried to get Cumeni back — it was a sore battle but none of the stripling sons died. Helaman's army fell on tough times, getting very little support. Helaman, Gid, and Teomner's armies took back the city of Manti.

Year 13 of the War Chapters (62 BC/30th Year of the Reign of the Judges): Moroni received an epistle from Helaman stating that they needed help. Moroni wrote to Pahoran asking for men to be sent to that part of the land so Helaman's armies could maintain their cities. No men were sent, and the Lamanites took over the land of Nephihah. Moroni focused on maintaining the other Nephite cities. He also sent an angry epistle to Pahoran, and Pahoran wrote back explaining that the king-men took his judgment-seat and he had fled to Gideon. Moroni took men to Gideon to help Pahoran. He raised the Title of Liberty everywhere and his army grew. Pachus, the king of the king-men was killed; Pahoran was put back in his judgment-seat; the king-men were no more; and peace was back in Zarahemla.

Year 14 of the War Chapters (61 BC/31st Year of the Reign of the Judges): Moroni sent provisions to Lehi, Helaman and Teancum. Moroni and Pahoran took back the city of Nephihah. Some Lamanite prisoners covenanted peace and joined with the people of Ammon. Moroni pursued the Lamanites from city to city until meeting up with Lehi and Teancum. They all got to the land of Moroni and surrounded the Lamanites. Teancum killed Ammoron and in turn was killed. Moroni drove the Lamanites out of the land of Moroni. The war was finally over.

Aftermath of the War Chapters (60-56BC/32nd-36th Year of the Reign of the Judges): Moroni fortified exposed Nephite lands, then went home and gave command of his army to his son, Moronihah, so he could retire. Pahoran returned to the judgment-seat, and Helaman and his brethren built up the church. The Nephites were strong, humble, and prosperous. Helaman died. Shiblon took possession of the sacred records. Moroni died.

Hymns About Being in God's Army

Sing these wonderful hymns with your family, friends, or alone, and imagine how you are a part of God's army.

Onward, Christian Soldiers

Verse 1:

Onward, Christian soldiers!
Marching as to war,
With the cross of Jesus
Going on before.
Christ, the royal Master,
Leads against the foe;
Forward into battle,
See his banners go!

(Chorus):

Onward, Christian soldiers!
Marching as to war,
With the cross of Jesus
Going on before.

Verse 2:

At the sign of triumph
Satan's host doth flee;

On, then, Christian soldiers
On to victory.
Hell's foundations quiver
At the shout of praise;
Brothers, lift your voices,
Loud your anthems raise.

Verse 3:

Like a mighty army
Moves the Church of God;
Brothers, we are treading
Where the Saints have trod.
We are not divided;
All one body we:
One in hope and doctrine,
One in charity.

Verse 4:

Onward, then, ye people;
Join our happy throng.
Blend with ours your voices
In the triumph song:
Glory, laud, and honor
Unto Christ, the King.
This through countless ages
Men and angels sing.

Text: Sabine Baring-Gould, 1834-1924

Music: Arthur S. Sullivan, 1842-1900 (*"Onward Christian Soldiers, Hymns, 1985, hymn 246*)

We Are all Enlisted

Verse 1:

We are all enlisted till the conflict is o'er;
Happy are we! Happy are we!
Soldiers in the army, there's a bright crown in store;
We shall win and wear it by and by.
Haste to the battle, quick to the field;
Truth is our helmet, buckler, and shield.
Stand by our colors; proudly they wave!
We're joyfully, joyfully marching to our home.

(Chorus)

We are all enlisted till the conflict is o'er;
Happy are we! Happy are we!
Soldiers in the army, there's a bright crown in store;
We shall win and wear it by and by.

Verse 2:

Hark! the sound of battle sounding loudly and clear;
Come join the ranks! Come join the ranks!
We are waiting now for soldiers; who'll volunteer?
Rally round the standard of the cross.
Hark! 'tis our Captain calls you today;
Lose not a moment, make no delay!
Fight for our Savior; come, come away!
We're joyfully, joyfully marching to our home.

Verse 3:

Fighting for a kingdom, and the world is our foe;
Happy are we! Happy are we!

Glad to join the army, we will sing as we go;
We shall gain the vict'ry by and by.
Dangers may gather — why should we fear?
Jesus, our Leader, ever is near.
He will protect us, comfort, and cheer.
We're joyfully, joyfully marching to our home.

Text: Anon., The New Golden Chain, New York, 1866
Music: William B. Bradbury, 1816-1868 (*"We Are All Enlisted," Hymns, 1985, hymn 250*)

100 Things the Book of Mormon has Taught Me

I want to share with you 100 beautiful truths from the Book of Mormon that have helped, and continue to help me, in my journey to be more like my Savior. Many of them are in the war chapters, but there are so many more! Enjoy using these in your scripture study.

1. The Lord provides a way for us to follow His commands (1 Nephi 3:7).
2. The Lord can do all things for us, that are His will, if we have faith in Him (1 Nephi 7:12).
3. Sometimes the Lord commands us to do things for a purpose we don't understand (1 Nephi 9:5).
4. If we listen to the word of God, and follow it, the devil can't overpower us (1 Nephi 15:24).
5. We receive strength as we obey God's commandments (1 Nephi 17:3).
6. Regardless of our afflictions, we should praise God and not murmur (1 Nephi 18:16).
7. Jesus Christ offered himself as a sacrifice for sin. Only through His mercy and grace, can those who believe return to God's presence (2 Nephi 2:6-8).
8. Everything must have its opposite. You cannot have one without the other (2 Nephi 2:11-13).
9. We all have our free agency to choose to follow Christ or the devil (2 Nephi 2:27, 2 Nephi 10:23).
10. Those who trust man instead of God are cursed (2 Nephi 4:34).
11. The Lord admonishes us to listen to Him and not

be afraid of men, for they die. The Lord and His righteousness are forever (2 Nephi 8:7-8, 12).

12. The Lord will bless you and give you knowledge if you are humble. He despises those who value riches and knowledge of men more than His counsel (2 Nephi 9:28-30, 42).

13. We are saved by grace after all we can do (2 Nephi 25:23).

14. People will say they have a bible and don't need another bible. The Lord answers by saying He loves His people all over the world and He will visit all nations after His resurrection. A written testimony of two nations is a witness of Him, and that He remembers all nations (2 Nephi 29:7-8).

15. The Lamb of God was holy, yet He was baptized to fulfill all righteousness. We who are unholy, must be baptized to show obedience to God and His commandments (2 Nephi 31:5-7).

16. After we are baptized, we still have work to do to receive eternal life. We must stay faithful, love God and our neighbors, follow the word of Christ, etc. (2 Nephi 31:19-20).

17. After we are baptized and receive the gift of the Holy Ghost, we can speak by the power of the Holy Ghost. As we study our scriptures, we will know what we should do (2 Nephi 32:2-3, 5).

18. Pray always. Don't do anything unto the Lord without praying first for help (2 Nephi 32:9).

19. Seek for the kingdom of God before you seek for riches. If you do obtain riches, use them to do good to others, for we are all precious to God (Jacob 2:18-21).

20. When we serve others, we are serving God. If we praise, thank, and serve God all our lives with our whole souls, we will still be unprofitable servants.

All we must do is keep His commandments, and we are blessed. We will always be indebted to Christ and have no reason to ever boast of ourselves (Mosiah 2:17, 20-24).

21. We must be like little children and put off the natural man, else we are an enemy to God (Mosiah 3:18-19).

22. God created all things, has all wisdom, and all power. We can't comprehend what He can (Mosiah 4:9).

23. We should teach our children to keep God's commandments and to love and serve others. We should not withhold our help from those who need it, saying they deserve what they get. We are all beggars and rely on God for all (Mosiah 4:14-19).

24. We must watch our thoughts, words, and deeds, and keep God's commandments, else we will perish (Mosiah 4:30).

25. When we are baptized, we make a covenant to be obedient to all of God's commands, all our lives. When we make this covenant, we are called the children of Christ. We must remember Him always. How can we know Him if we do not serve Him and keep Him in our hearts? (Mosiah 5:5-13).

26. When we are baptized, we promise to mourn and comfort others and to stand as witnesses of God at all times and in all things and in all places (Mosiah 18:9).

27. The Lord will forgive those who repent. We should forgive each other as well. If we don't, then we will not be forgiven of our sins (Mosiah 26:30-31).

28. The judgments of God are always just, but the judgments of man are not (Mosiah 29:12).

29. Alma asks many questions to see if his people are prepared for salvation. These are great questions to

ponder and see how you are doing in your path of righteousness (Alma 5:14-32).

30. The word of God must be fulfilled, regardless of if people reject it (Alma 5:58).

31. To walk blameless before God, we must be humble, submissive, gentle, patient, long-suffering, temperate, diligent, grateful, and have faith, hope, and charity (Alma 7:23-24).

32. Christ has loosed the bands of temporal death. All will be resurrected (Alma 11:43-44).

33. Those with soft hearts receive more of God's word than those who harden their hearts (Alma 12:10).

34. This life is a time to prepare to meet God (Alma 12:24).

35. Do not procrastinate the day of your repentance, but instead watch and pray continually and have faith, and a hope of eternal life (Alma 13:27-30).

36. Who can glory too much in the Lord? (Alma 26:16).

37. God is mindful of all people and is merciful unto them (Alma 26:37).

38. What profit is it to labor in a church if you don't get paid? It is to rejoice in the joy of others (Alma 30:34-35).

39. All things denote there is a God (Alma 30:44).

40. The Lord provides strength, comfort, and patience to those who suffer afflictions, if they pray in faith (Alma 31:30-38).

41. It is better to humble yourself because of God's word than to be compelled to be humble (Alma 32:12-16).

42. Faith is not to have a perfect knowledge, but a hope for things which are not seen, which are true (Alma 32:21).

43. Faith begins with a desire to believe. Alma the younger, a prophet, compares the word of God unto a seed and explains how it can grow and bring forth fruit to you (Alma 32:27-43).

44. By small and simple things God brings about great things, including the salvation of souls (Alma 37:6-7).

45. The Lord keeps His promises, and always has (Alma 37:17).

46. If you counsel with the Lord, He will direct you. Those who pray daily and have hearts filled with gratitude daily will be lifted up at the last day (Alma 37:37).

47. You cannot hide your crimes from God. You must repent of your sins (Alma 39:8).

48. Do not seek after riches, for you can't take them with you (Alma 39:14).

49. Wickedness never was happiness. Those who do not follow God cannot be happy (Alma 41:10-11).

50. Christ's atonement has brought about the plan of mercy and appeases the demands of justice by allowing us to repent of our sins (Alma 42:13-15).

51. War is justified to protect families, lands, rights, and religion (Alma 43:46-47).

52. God will preserve the faithful. The Lord will not allow a people to be destroyed unless they fall into transgression and deny their faith (Alma 44:4).

53. Captain Moroni's character is explained, and then the prophet Mormon wrote that if all people were like him, the devil could have no power over anyone (Alma 48:11-13, 17).

54. If you do not doubt, God will deliver you from your enemies (Alma 56:47-48).

55. Joy and pureness of heart comes from humility and giving your heart to God (Helaman 3:35).

56. If you build your foundation on the rock of Christ, the devil cannot drag you down into misery and despair. Those who build a sure foundation cannot fall (Helaman 5:12).

57. Samuel, a Lamanite prophet, prophesies that the night before Christ is born, there will be no darkness, but a day and a night and a day of only light. A new star will arise, and signs and wonders will come from Heaven (Helaman 14:3-6).

58. Jesus must die so that the dead can be resurrected. His death redeems mankind and, through repentance, allows all to enter back into the presence of God (Helaman 14: 15-18).

59. Samuel prophesies that upon Christ's death, there will be darkness until He is resurrected. During this period of darkness, there will be terrible natural disasters, changing the face of the whole earth, above and beneath (Helaman 14:20-27).

60. The words of the prophets are fulfilled every whit (3 Nephi 1:20).

61. Christ extends His mercy to all who come to Him (3 Nephi 9:14).

62. Heavenly Father speaks to the Nephites in the land Bountiful and testifies of His beloved son. Jesus descends out of heaven and stands in their midst. He speaks of his atoning sacrifice and invites the multitude to thrust their hands into His side and feel the prints in His hands and feet (3 Nephi 11:7-15).

63. Jesus instructs the prophet Nephi on how baptism should be done - in His name, having proper authority, and by immersion (3 Nephi 11:21-26).

64. Contention and anger are of the devil (3 Nephi 11:29-30).

65. Jesus speaks the Beatitudes to the Nephites, just

as He did at the Sermon on the Mount (3 Nephi 12:3-12).
66. The Father knows what you need before you ask Him (3 Nephi 13:8).
67. If you first seek the kingdom of Heaven, you will be blessed with your temporal needs (3 Nephi 13:33).
68. Do not judge others. First look at yourself and what you need to change before you point out others' faults (3 Nephi 14:1-5).
69. Only those who do the will of the Father will enter the kingdom of Heaven (3 Nephi 14:21).
70. When Christ told the Jews that He had other sheep which were not of this fold, they thought He meant the Gentiles. However, Jesus tells the Nephites that this is not so; that the other sheep are them and other people around the world that He would visit after His resurrection (3 Nephi 15:16-24).
71. Just as in His mortal ministry, Jesus, full of compassion, heals the sick. He then blesses the children one by one and prays for them. Angels descend out of heaven and minister to the little ones (3 Nephi 17:6-25).
72. Jesus ordains a disciple with power to bless and administer the bread and wine to all those who are baptized in His name. Partaking of the bread and wine shows Heavenly Father that we remember Jesus and keep His commandments. He promises that if the people remember Him, they will always have His Spirit to be with them. Those who partake worthily of these emblems are built upon His rock (3 Nephi 18:5-12).
73. Jesus commands us to watch and pray always to avoid temptation. Satan wants to overtake us. Anything we ask the Father in Christ's name will be given to us if we ask in faith, and it is God's will.

Jesus commands us to pray in our families (3 Nephi 18:15-21).

74. Jesus says to meet together often and to accept all people into the congregation of the church. Pray for them. Set an example for them, as He has set for us (3 Nephi 18:22-24).

75. The words of Isaiah are great, and all things that he prophesied have been and shall be (3 Nephi 23:1-3).

76. Jesus Christ's church should bear His name, and should be built upon His gospel, or else it be another man's church (3 Nephi 27:3-8).

77. All will be judged by Jesus Christ according to their works. All who repent, are baptized, and endure to the end will be held guiltless before Heavenly Father on judgment day (3 Nephi 27:13-17).

78. We should do what Jesus would and did do. We should be like Him (3 Nephi 27:21, 27).

79. The way to eternal life is straight and narrow. Few will find it (3 Nephi 27:33).

80. The judgments of God will overtake the wicked. The wicked punish the wicked by stirring them up to desire bloodshed. (Mormon 4:5).

81. The Book of Mormon shall be hidden until the Lord sees fit for it to be brought forth. Its purpose will be to persuade the House of Israel that Jesus is the Christ, the son of God (Mormon 5:12-14).

82. God has all power, and at His command anything can come to pass (Mormon 5:23).

83. Mormon invites the Lamanites of the latter days to repent, to be baptized and to take hold of the gospel of Christ, set forth in the Bible and the Book of Mormon. The Book of Mormon is written to help people believe in the Bible. If you believe the Bible,

you will believe the Book of Mormon too (Mormon 7:8-9).

84. Moroni prophesies about the coming forth of the Book of Mormon. It will only be able to come forth by the power of God by one whose eye is single to His glory. It shall come forth in a time where people no longer believe in miracles, when churches and teachers are lifted up in pride, when there are wars and rumors of wars, great pollutions and sin upon the earth, etc. (Mormon 8:14-33).

85. Miracles have not ceased. Because God is the same yesterday, today and forever, miracles still happen for the faithful who trust in God. Those who do not doubt can pray to Heavenly Father and He will answer their prayers. (Mormon 9:15-21).

86. The promised land (the Americas) will be free from bondage from all other nations if its people serve Jesus Christ (Ether 2:9-10, 12).

87. Anything that persuades to do good is from God (Ether 4:12).

88. Do not say something doesn't exist because you can't see it or have proof. You will not receive a witness until after your faith is tried (Ether 12: 6).

89. Miracles only occur when one first has faith in the son of God (Ether 12:12-18).

90. God gives us weakness so we will be humble. If we are humble and have faith, God will make our weaknesses strengths (Ether 12:27).

91. In the church of Christ, members will fellowship each other and help each other keep the faith. They will meet often to fast, pray, help each other, and to partake of the Sacrament in remembrance of the Lord, Jesus Christ (Moroni 6:4-6).

92. A good person will do good things. When offering a gift or praying, we must do so with real

intent to do good (Moroni 7: 5-10).

93. All things of God invite one to do good. We all have been given the light of Christ, which helps us discern between good and evil. The devil never persuades anyone to do good (Moroni 7:12-17).

94. We must have charity. It is the pure love of Christ, and never fails. We must pray to the Father to be filled with His love and be like Christ (Moroni 7:45-48).

95. Little children are not capable of committing sin. They are not accountable and need no repentance. Thus, they do not need to be baptized. They are alive in Christ (Moroni 8).

96. Perfect love removes all fear (Moroni 8:16).

97. As we are forgiven of our sins, we become gentler and not easily offended. With these traits, we are filled with the Holy Ghost, which brings hope and perfect love. This love can endure through diligent prayer (Moroni 8:26).

98. Moroni promises that those who ask Heavenly Father in sincere, faithful prayer if the Book of Mormon is true, will receive an answer through the Holy Ghost, who testifies of all truth (Moroni 10:4-5).

99. God has given us many different spiritual gifts. They are manifested to us by the Holy Spirit to help us and others draw closer to Christ (Moroni 10:8-18).

100. If we come unto Christ and deny ourselves of all ungodliness, loving the Lord with all our hearts, we can be perfected and made holy through His grace (Moroni 10:32-33).

This is by no means an all-inclusive list. There are hundreds, if not thousands, of precious truths we can pull from this perfect book. Throughout it, we read of prophets of God who were courageous, bold, true, always obedient, filled with love for their brethren, all having a pure love of God and a desire to share His light and gospel with others.

The most perfect example from the Book of Mormon is Jesus Christ Himself. The words He spoke to the Nephite people whom He visited in the Americas following His resurrection, are of supreme value.

As I went through the Book of Mormon's 531 pages, making this list, I was overwhelmed with how often Jesus Christ is mentioned, praised, prophesied of, and reverenced. The Book of Mormon truly is a companion to the Bible - another testament of Jesus Christ. I know it is true.

Of all the self-help books you could ever choose to read, choose The Book of Mormon.

Sources

- King James Version Bible (2013). KJV Online. https://www.churchofjesuschrist.org/study/scriptures?lang=eng&platform=web
- The Book of Mormon (2013). BOM Online. https://www.churchofjesuschrist.org/study/scriptures?lang=eng&platform=web
- Spencer W. Kimball, in Conference Report, Apr. 1978, 117; or Ensign, May 1978, 77
- Harold B. Lee, "Feet Shod with the Preparation of the Gospel of Peace," Brigham Young University Speeches of the Year [Nov. 9, 1954], 2–3, 6–7
- Gordon B. Hinckley, in Conference Report, Apr. 2003, 83–84; or Ensign, May 2003, 80
- Bruce R. McConkie, Mormon Doctrine, 2nd ed. [1966], 805
- George Albert Smith, Teachings of Presidents of the Church: George Albert Smith, Chapter 18
- Paul E. Koelliker, "Gospel Covenants Bring Promised Blessings," Ensign or Liahona, Nov. 2005, 94
- President Joseph Fielding Smith, The Way to Perfection [1970], 121
- Elaine S Dalton, "A Return to Virtue," General Conference, October 2008
- Robert D. Hales, "Christian Courage: The Price of Discipleship," Ensign or Liahona, Nov. 2008, 74
- Neal A. Maxwell, Men and Women of Christ [1991], 4

- Russell M. Nelson, in Conference Report, Apr. 1989, 86–88; or Ensign, May 1989, 68, 70
- James E. Faust, "Be Not Afraid," Ensign, Oct. 2002, 4
- Dallin H. Oaks, "World Peace," Ensign, May 1990
- Henry B. Eyring, "Always," Ensign, Oct. 1999
- Ezra Taft Benson, The Teachings of Ezra Taft Benson [1988], 285
- David A. Bednar, "Watchful unto Prayer Continually," Ensign, Nov. 2019
- President Joseph F. Smith, Improvement Era, Sept. 1914, pp. 1074–75
- Ronald A. Rasband, "Build a Fortress of Spirituality and Protection," General Conference, April 2019
- Neal A. Maxwell, That My Family Should Partake [1974], 58–59
- Hugh Nibley, Since Cumorah, 2nd ed. [1988], 339–40
- Joseph Smith, Teachings of Presidents of the Church: Joseph Smith, 214
- Gordon B., "Prophet Grateful for Gospel, Testimony," Church News,21, 1996, 4
- Russell M. Nelson, "Face the Future with Faith," Ensign or Liahona, May 2011, 34
- Gene R. Cook, Receiving Answers to Our Prayers [1996], 156–57
- Dennis E. Simmons, in Conference Report, Apr. 1997, 41–42; or Ensign, May 1997, 31
- Heber J. Grant, J. Reuben Clark Jr., and David O. McKay, in Conference Report, Apr. 1942, 95–96

- Orson F. Whitney, Life of Heber C. Kimball [1945], 64
- Dallin H. Oaks, "Adversity," BYU Speech, January 17, 1995
- Boyd K. Packer, "The Mystery of Life," Ensign, Nov. 1983, 18
- Thomas S Monson, "The Call for Courage," General Conference, April 2004
- Gary E. Stevenson, "Be Valiant in Courage, Strength, and Activity," Ensign, November 2012
- Richard J. Maynes, "The Strength to Endure," Ensign, November 2013
- Joseph B. Wirthlin, "True to the Truth," Ensign, May 1997
- James J. Hamula, "Winning the War against Evil," Ensign, November 2008
- Thomas S. Monson, "Keep the Commandments, Ensign, November 2015
- Ruth B. Wright, "Teaching Children to Walk Uprightly Before the Lord," Ensign, May 1994
- Miriam-Webster dictionary, https://www.merriam-webster.com/
- Ezra Taft Benson, in Conference Report, Oct. 1962, 14–15
- Brian K Taylor, "Am I a Child of God?," Ensign, May 2018
- Rex C. Reeve, "Look to God," Ensign, November 1982
- Robert D. Hales, "Preserving Agency, Protecting Religious Freedom," Ensign, May 2015

- Ezra Taft Benson, "Our Immediate Responsibility," Conference Report, p. 120, October 1966
- Dallin H Oaks, "World Peace." Ensign, May 1990
- John A. Widtsoe, in Conference Report, Oct. 1943, p. 113
- M. Russell Ballard, "Let Our Voices Be Heard," Ensign or Liahona, Nov. 2003, 18
- W. Douglas Shumway, "Marriage and Family: Our Sacred Responsibility," Ensign, May 2004
- Boyd K. Packer, in Conference Report, Oct. 1990, 107–8; or Ensign, Nov. 1990, 84
- "Oath and Covenant of the Priesthood,"https://www.churchofjesuschrist.org/study/scriptures/gs/oath-and-covenant-of-the-priesthood?lang=eng
- David A. Bednar, "And Nothing Shall Offend Them," Ensign or Liahona, Nov. 2006, 91–92
- L. Tom Perry, "The Power of Deliverance," Ensign, May 2012
- Glenn L. Pace, in Conference Report, Oct. 1990, 8; or Ensign, Nov. 1990, 8–9
- Jeffrey R. Holland, "Mormon: The Man and the Book, Part I," Ensign, 1978
- Russell M. Nelson, www.ldsliving.com, Aug. 29, 2019
- Neal A. Maxwell, in Conference Report, Apr. 2002, 43; or Ensign, May 2002, 37
- Ray H. Wood, in Conference Report, Apr. 1999, 54; or Ensign, May 1999, 40–41
- Dean L. Larsen, "Likening the Scriptures unto Us," in Monte S. Nyman and Charles D. Tate

Jr., eds., Alma, the Testimony of the Word [1992], 8
- Neal A. Maxwell, "Repentance," Ensign, October 1991
- Ezra Taft Benson, The Teachings of Ezra Taft Benson [1988], 72
- Neal A. Maxwell, in Conference Report, Oct. 1991, 40; or Ensign, Nov. 1991, 31
- Spencer W. Kimball, The Miracle of Forgiveness [1969], 117
- Gordon B. Hinckley, "The War We Are Winning," Ensign, Nov. 1986, 42, 44–45)
- "Onward Christian Soldiers, Hymns, 1985, hymn 246
- "We Are All Enlisted," Hymns, 1985, hymn 250

Acknowledgements

I'm so grateful to my Heavenly Parents for blessing me with the gift of writing. I'm grateful that I had the opportunity to teach a class that would change my spiritual understanding forever, and I'm grateful that the Holy Ghost prompted me to write this book.

I thank my family and friends for believing in me and supporting me through this long process, especially my cousin Brooke who was the first person to read my book three years ago in its earliest draft form. She gave me encouraging feedback which helped give me the confidence to move forward.

This book would not be nearly as polished and complete without the help of many special friends who read the whole draft and provided wonderful suggestions for improvement: Brandi, Judy, Savanna, and Kathie. Most of all I must thank Tina, who tirelessly helped me with readability and formatting, and Jess, who gave me such beautiful feedback all the way through and diligently and excitedly created my amazing book cover.

It takes a village to make art happen and I'm forever thankful for mine.

About the Author

Mandy Al-Bjaly has always loved reading, writing, and teaching, so writing this book just made sense. She lives in Mebane, NC with her wonderful Jordanian husband and most of her five children (her oldest is currently a missionary). Mandy loves bringing people together in friendship and laughter and strives to inspire, uplift, and help others as much as she can. In her free time, which is rare these days, she likes to go thrifting, spend time with friends and family, take walks, or do something musical like sing showtunes. She has written a blog since 2014 at www.ablisscomplete.com. Check out her post called "The Enemy" for a tie-in to Captain Moroni!

If you like my book, please leave a review. I would be so grateful!